Cosmic
Guidance
for
Mastering Your Life

Cosmic Guidance

for
Mastering Your Life

Daily Notes

Eleanor Haspel-Portner Ph.D.

Cosmic Guidance for Mastering Your Life: Daily Notes

Library of Congress Control Number:
2023923470

ISBN:
978-1-931053-11-2 (Paperback)
978-1-931053-12-9 (Paperback)

BODY, MIND & SPIRIT / Inspiration & Personal Growth
SELF-HELP / Journaling
HEALTH & FITNESS / Alternative Therapies

Other titles by Eleanor Haspel-Portner
Cosmic Secrets
Astrology Essentials
First Degree Reiki Manual
Second Degree Reiki Manual & Workbook
Marriage in Trouble: A Time of Decision

Author's websites
www.nobleenergywellness.com
www.DrEleanor.com
www.moptu.com/DrEleanor

Book Design by Michelle M. White
Illustration by Katikam at stock.adobe.com.

Noble Energy Wellness

To Marvin, my husband and soul mate,
your love and support bless me abundantly.
And to all who seek self-knowledge
and have the inner knowing and courage
to pursue the depth of consciousness.

Table of Contents

From the Author

You are here to manifest who you are at the depth of your soul. Your life is governed by four dimensions, or Four Worlds: the Mental World, the Spiritual World, the Emotional World, and the Physical World. Each World operates in a different energetic frequency to motivate you toward manifesting in different energies in the world of reality. *Cosmic Guidance for Mastering Your Life* offers you daily guidance in the Four Worlds and also in the Integrated World in which you function, most likely, as a Manifesting Generator (someone who envisions what they want and can manifest it).

The Mental World is the most familiar World to you. It is the world of your reality functioning, meaning your intellectual awareness of how to do things and how to live in your culture. You learn how to be a good citizen, how to study, how to dress, and how to earn money. Day-to-day life is generally lived primarily in your conscious awake life. Most astrology and psychology work occurs primarily at the Mental level of your awareness and thus ignores what may, in fact, be most empowering and exciting to you at a deep level of your soul.

The Spiritual World is the unifying integrating world of consciousness. It is at your soul level that you know who you are and what is right for you in your life. When you are at peace with your inner core, you feel joyful and alive. Your sense of Self comes from this level of your being, and it is here that you truly want to be acknowledged and loved.

When you sleep, you move into the collective unconscious, where all knowledge and acceptance exist. During the first three months of your life, you are more anchored in your spiritual core and in your emotional responses than in your Mental World. This is because the cortex of your brain is still developing and needs stimulation from outside the womb to trigger physical responses that hook up neurologically to associative areas of your brain. In other words, during the first three months of your life, you are being wired up by cosmic and environmental energy frequencies that you respond to in your own way. By the time you are three months old, you have developed preferences for certain kinds of energy patterns and dislikes for other kinds of energy patterns.

It is only when your Mental World comes under your conscious control that you begin to exercise your Free Choice. As a baby, when you begin to reach for objects and have dominion over how you express what you want, you begin to experience yourself as who you are.

Humans have the capacity for self-reflection and growth. Self-reflection requires discipline, time, and a willingness to think outside your usual patterns and pathways in each of the Four Worlds. As a practicing psychologist for over 50 years, and with my background in multiple disciplines that broaden the scope of my thinking, I have observed that recognizing that you live in multiple dimensions or frequencies and that each of these Worlds has its own rules, ways of communicating, and purpose in your consciousness facilitates wise choices and leads to empowered actions.

When I began to work with the Kabalistic Tree of Life, I recognized the importance of including the Worlds when thinking about the process of Individuation (self-growth; fulfillment). It is only when you integrate all components of your life, that your spiritual core as the overseer of your destiny and life path becomes your true compass and guiding star.

One of the ways I validated the benefits of using the Noble Energy Maps System was to write statements in each world for each day of the year. At first, I was curious about whether Noble Energy Maps would tell me enough to give me guidance on the day. To my surprise and delight, not only did the statements I wrote guide me, but they even alerted me to the energy I would encounter in ways that no other astrologically based system had ever done. I even traded the stock market based on the energy of the day.

After several years, I stopped writing Cosmic Guidance statements and focused on other areas of my work. However, in October 2022, as I stood doing Tai Chi Gung Figure 8's at my husband's bedside while listening to a Jim Goure prayer, I was instructed by the Holy Spirit to release my work to the public and to focus on the Four Worlds and on the Integrated World. In that moment, I knew the importance of living in the Integrated World with awareness of how the Mental, Spiritual, Emotional, and Physical Worlds feed our energy and impact our responses.

How to Use this Book

This book, *Cosmic Guidance for Mastering your Life*, alerts you to the energy of each day in each World: Mental, Spiritual, Emotional, and Physical. Each statement focuses on the energy frequency of the World on that day and how you might orient yourself in a way that aligns you optimally in that world. For example, on a day when strong manifesting energy occurs but only in the Mental World, I might advise you that outside pressure may push you toward action, but because the energy comes from outside of you rather than from inside of you, it might then be wise to wait for the outside energy to pass so your decision is more centered within yourself.

Because each world has its own energy frequency, I have color coded the worlds by their astrologically associated colors as taught in Kabalistic Tree of Life. The Mental World is yellow, the Emotional World is blue green, the Spiritual World is purple, and the Physical World is red orange. The Integrated World is grey. Each world also has its own way of communicating and listening for how the different ways you know and feel can put you in touch with each of the worlds and how you know what you know.

Each statement is designed for a particular day of the year. Begin your journal on the appropriate date, and when you get to the end, return to January 1. To make *Daily Cosmic Guidance for Mastering Your Life* most effective for you, read the day's statements each morning before you start your busy day. Consider taking a photo of the statements to refer to them throughout the day as a way to affirm balance internally when you need it. If you have time during your day, jot down any ideas or observations that advance your thinking and consciousness. At the end of your day, review the statements for the day and reflect on them.

- What worked for you?
- What would you like to do differently?
- What did you learn about yourself today?

Each page has a section for notes. If you like to write more, use a second journal, and make a note of the date before you write so you can go back to the statements later to assess their value and guidance.

You will find that I frequently recommend other resources that may help center or align you energetically in the Cosmic Guidance statements. These resources will be italicized throughout the book, and are listed on page 373 with a QR code directing you to a web page where they can be found (https://www.nobleenergywellness.com/cosmic-guidance/).

Let's embark on this journey together to help you discover the key to a life of fulfillment and the recognition of your divine essence.

In Loving Light,
Dr. Eleanor
Mount Pleasant, South Carolina
October 2023

Daily Guidance
&
Evening Reflections

January 1, _____

Mental
Stay in touch with your inner alignment, and trust your perceptions before you trust the perceptions of others.

Spiritual
When inner challenges come to light, they inspire new goals.

Emotional
Inner power comes through intuition.

Physical
You are physically sensitive today. Thus, those you are with may affect you.

Integration
Tension comes from wanting to find what is truly important or meaningful to you. Tune in to yourself long enough to feel secure that you know what feels good. Take your time instead of rushing. Surround yourself only with those you trust or with whom you feel truly comfortable, otherwise, you may get pulled into things you later have to revise or struggle to change. While experiences call to you, getting involved in too many things may pull you away from your focus and may lead you in directions you later find uncomfortable. Take your time to relax. Until inner tension dissolves, do nothing. Your mind needs time to decipher information in a way you can grasp it.

Evening Reflection: My Insights from Today

January 2, _____

Mental
Question things and consider creative ideas, but avoid decisions.

Spiritual
Anxiety or fears tell you if you are in alignment.

Emotional
Tap into your depth of inner knowing, and use your senses for information.

Physical
Be aware of your sensitivities
and take on only what leaves you energy to spare.

Integration
Tension beneath the surface of your actions drives you in ways that may provoke you and others. Yet, despite your desire and attempts to describe your feelings, you may not be able to put your finger on your perceptions and you may feel misunderstood. With your intuition strong in the moment, over time you will begin to get a sense for what it was that you were thinking. Ideas today, however, may elude your understanding. You need incubation time before trying to communicate to others. You know much more than you can say and do; be gentle on yourself, and stay in quiet places where others will not influence your feelings about yourself.

Evening Reflection: My Insights from Today

January 3, _____

Mental
Questions that you ask now require contemplation before action.
Mental overload is possible.

Spiritual
Tune in to others by watching your body's reactions.

Emotional
Inner power comes through intuition.

Physical
You are highly sensitive and empathic.
Conserve your energy by being sensitive to yourself.

Integration
With internal tension at a high today, use your inner resources in economical ways. Balance what you tell yourself about your needs and wants. Tension continues to push you toward inner understanding of your vulnerabilities. Thus, you might question many aspects of your life. You may feel overwhelmed by the pressures of family or work and want to escape from what people project on you. While you think your instincts have basis, you also pick up on collective feelings unconsciously and from deep within yourself when you sleep. These feelings coupled with your inner tensions may push you toward precipitous action that could waste your resources, financial, and otherwise. Avoid any action or any decisions today unless they were initiated in the past and only come to fruition today. Wait until inner tensions ease and clarity of your inner purpose feel more in harmony.

Evening Reflection: My Insights from Today

January 4, _____

Mental
Imagine possibilities and how they can come true.
Listen for your inner voice.

Spiritual
Listen to what your body tells you about the effect others have on you.

Emotional
Balancing the *Axes of Awareness* (see resources on page 373) is key
in staying balanced.

Physical
Do less than you think you can and be certain to take time to rest.

Integration
Struggling with issues that challenge the very depth of your life purpose have
the potential to bring you consciousness and self-awareness in a whole new
way. While you know what you believe you know, it is essential to confirm
your knowing with factual outcomes over time. Avoid coming to any conclusions about the workings of your inner Self. Listen for the voice of inner
wisdom and trust the inner teacher who guides you toward dominion of the
Self over the personality. Time is your friend.

Evening Reflection: My Insights from Today

January 5, _____

Mental
Make sure you honor what you know is right for you.
You are vulnerable to input from other people.

Spiritual
Stay open to the way what you envision feels spiritually,
and allow it to guide you.

Emotional
Make sure your mind honors your instincts.
Respect and acknowledge all aspects of yourself.

Physical
Pressure toward action may put you under stress.
Take your time and remember to breathe deeply and relax.

Integration
Things begin to feel more solid as things start to make some sense. Ideas and associations from the past may fall into the context of what has been going on. You still may not feel like you know your direction, focus, or how to fully comprehend what has been happening in the wider scheme of things. Trust that time nurtures your ambitions, and your imagination will eventually come together with circumstances to fill in some details.

Evening Reflection: My Insights from Today

January 6, _____

Mental
Energy follows thought.
Stay true to what you know aligns with your highest Self.

Spiritual
Listen to what your body tells you about the effect others have on you.

Emotional
Use your inner power to be aware of your feelings on all levels.

Physical
Be watchful and careful with your physical exertion today.

Integration
Use your intuition and instincts to sensitively tune in to situations that may be unhealthy for you on a subtle level. Pay attention to where you are as well as what you are there for; pay attention to your emotionality. Remember past experiences that can help modulate current choices about where you go and what you expose yourself to. Be careful about those people you have around you. Choices you make set in motion events that impact you in the future.

Evening Reflection: My Insights from Today

January 7, _____

Mental
Stay true to your intuitive Self
even when you do not understand your reasons.

Spiritual
You know more than you think you know. Take time to listen.

Emotional
Avoid any emotional confrontations.

Physical
Rest more than usual and listen to your body's signals.
Avoid overexertion.

Integration
Emotions are tricky to navigate when different components of you tell you different things. It is always important to make no assumptions or judgments without checking out the facts and their source. Only take as true what you have considered carefully and without distortion of your beliefs. Imagine how each scenario you imagine will play out and ask, "Is this what I want to have happen?" Everyone is being driven by their own agenda, so take drama in your life with a "grain of salt." Remain balanced despite challenges.

Evening Reflection: My Insights from Today

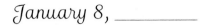

January 8, _____

Mental
Keep an open mind so you can listen to your intuitions as they grow with you.

Spiritual
Listen to your inner voice of wisdom so you claim your own power.

Emotional
When provoked by emotions, breathe deeply,
relax, and wait to feel balance.

Physical
Pay special attention to your physical health. Optimize it.

Integration
Remain true to your inner connection to your Higher Self as you listen carefully for what intuitively makes sense (often your inner voice is a whisper). Emotions may eventually emerge out of seeds you plant in the now. Remember that all beings are interconnected and honor that connection. You are linked on the collective unconscious level of your being and have a deep relationship to everyone else at that level. Honor this unity by remaining mentally open despite the effort it takes. Change thought patterns in the interest of allowing new feelings to link you to others as you feel and express gratitude for the gifts of life.

Evening Reflection: My Insights from Today

January 9, _____

Mental
Actively visualize balance in your health and life.

Spiritual
Listen to your inner voice when you respond in your environment.

Emotional
Keep still when you feel any stress so you can access its source intuitively.

Physical
Start or re-commit to a program for improving your health.

Integration
Focus on inner transformation of instinctive feelings that arise in your daily life. Respond to circumstances with compassionate understanding rather than from raw animal instinct. When your instinct tells you what you want to achieve and how you can go about achieving it, project into future circumstances, consider other people and your inner direction, i.e., all conditions of your inner and outer reality prior to actually responding. Since life is an unfolding process, this kind of consideration must always be applied. Your sensitivity is part of an interconnected consciousness that serves the whole. Allow your inner Self to remain open without judgment until you know clearly your own direction.

Evening Reflection: My Insights from Today

January 10, _____

Mental

Watch your attitudes and ideas, monitoring them with alertness.

Spiritual

Tap into your depth of awareness
so your inner wisdom and strength directs you.

Emotional

Keep emotions in check so you remain
on an even keel today despite the unexpected.

Physical

Future health is programmed strongly today.
Pay extra attention to your body.

Integration

Inner connections about yourself in terms of "the big picture" may begin to surface. Let your personal history find expression in how you view yourself. Tune in to subtle feelings that point to your higher purpose or the role you play in the greater whole even though you cannot yet fully grasp what it is. Be patient. Set *SMART Goals* (see resources on page 373). Stay in touch with your own core, and do not make more promises than you can easily keep. Do not push yourself.

Evening Reflection: My Insights from Today

_____

_____

_____

_____

_____

_____

_____

_____

_____

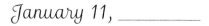

January 11, _____

Mental
Observe how your thinking shifts as you interact with others.

Spiritual
Stay focused on your goals, and meditate on
how to live according to them.

Emotional
Keep your power instead of giving it to others.

Physical
Remain alert to your body's responses. They speak strongly to you.

Integration
Emphasize connecting your body to your Higher Self by recognizing your body as a vehicle of consciousness. Your body connects multiple complex variations within itself and to others. Undertake new projects about which you feel ambitious that relate to your health, e.g., a new eating plan, a new approach to or design of your living space, a new way of gathering together with family and friends while dining or meditating. Take this opportunity to begin something that you will most likely experience in three months as having empowered you in ways you had not expected. Pick something that can integrate mind and body and something about which you feel passion. Seize this moment.

Evening Reflection: My Insights from Today

January 12, _____

Mental
Be patient while you seek insights
and a mental grasp on questions you have.

Spiritual
Take time to meditate so you stay in touch with your inner still point.

Emotional
Balancing the *Axes of Awareness* (see resources on page 373) is critical in finding your emotional center. Wait for balance and inner clarity.

Physical
Exercise moderation in all physical areas today.

Integration
The quest for understanding yourself and the world around you is important in how you orient to challenges. Pay special attention to your goals and to the questions you ask yourself about them. Acknowledge your achievements and process in moving toward your goals. What forward movement have you already made in your wisdom and understanding? What would you like to have happen next? Remember that you are able to manifest in the world when you tap into the power of your integrated Self. You are designed to participate in your life as an active instrument, making your own music and hearing your own inner voice. Listen and live your unique life.

Evening Reflection: My Insights from Today

_____

_____

_____

_____

_____

_____

_____

_____

January 13, _____

Mental
Input from others may confuse you about what you want.

Spiritual
When in doubt, consider what you know and relate well to based on past experiences.

Emotional
When you stay in touch with your own needs, you can be emotionally clearer with other people.

Physical
Be disciplined in your eating, exercising, and meditating.

Integration
It is natural to want to make sense out of things you experience as well as to feel puzzled at times by your life issues. Understanding takes patience; allow yourself time to take things in. Consider your goals, ambitions, and feelings. Your reactions to things and to people change with your situation and environment. It is more important to flow with your own values of interconnectedness rather than imposing something from the past on yourself. As you find yourself increasingly where you need to be at the right time, you may find that the environment in which you move changes as well; you may find a better fit to your own needs, wants, and desires. Give yourself time to feel your own individual instincts without acting impulsively on them. Take time to consider your values.

Evening Reflection: My Insights from Today

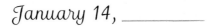

January 14, _____

Mental
Think deeply about what you want
with the intention of setting clear future goals.

Spiritual
You need time alone today in order to hear the inner voice
that speaks in whispers and guides you along your divine path.

Emotional
Draw on your past social intelligence in communications.

Physical
Get plenty of rest. Use your breathing as an indicator of stress.

Integration
Most individuals become manifesting generators when they function consciously. What this means is that alert inner awareness is essential for intentions to play out in alignment to your highest goals. Things in your life and in the world become clear over time. Consider what is at stake and what your values are. Continue to listen to your inner voice, so when external forces come together for you, you take proper action. Your mind/body program continues to ground you while building your strength. Continue to trust that the cosmic program is doing its work; and remember, it is natural to feel discouragement from time to time.

Evening Reflection: My Insights from Today

January 15, _____

Mental

Remain patient with your process until you find the approach to situations and people that puts you at ease.

Spiritual

Stay within your comfort zone while considering new options.

Emotional

Sensitivity to others may require you to rise above your feelings. Listen to yourself and use your instincts intelligently.

Physical

Overexertion may be depleting.

Integration

You may feel some conflicting things today. On the one hand, you might feel a bit discouraged about your desire to be clear on your direction; on the other hand, you may feel closer within yourself to proceeding in achieving your goals. You often need time for things to "simmer" within. The climate or context in which things happen or in which you find yourself are crucial for you. Be cognizant of the people around you and how they influence your self-feelings. Put yourself in the way of those with whom you are comfortable. Take yourself out of situations in which you are uncomfortable. Use this time to assess your situation further and prepare for the future.

Evening Reflection: My Insights from Today

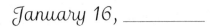

January 16, _____

Mental
Your thinking shapes your future.
Pay attention to the story you create and live.

Spiritual
Remain open to all possibilities for your future.

Emotional
Stay within your own limits to master yourself.

Physical
Actively visualize balance in your health and life.

Integration
Intuitive activity with inner knowing activates awareness and a sense of the importance of taking steps to assure that you are in a healthy situation for yourself. It is the things that support who you are and what you want to accomplish that can make this day shine for you. Ask for what you want if the moment feels appropriate, but wait if you have doubts. Any doubts that you consider tell you to wait. Within a couple of days your instincts that arise from today will clarify and provide you the broader picture of your sense of inner knowing. Such information confirms that you are on the right track. Hang tight despite your doubts and fears. It is a time for planting, not harvesting. Be wary of those who do not understand what you are striving for.

Evening Reflection: My Insights from Today

January 17, _____

Mental
Being true to yourself is crucial in reaching your highest goals.

Spiritual
Use words carefully.
Inner self-talk creates your intentions and their manifestation.

Emotional
Your words impact others.
Think before you speak, and speak honestly with sensitivity.

Physical
Pushing your body is unwise.

Integration
Values are an important key to who you are and what your life purpose drives you toward. When you are in alignment with your inner Self, this drive is clearer. When you release tension around you from those who limit your inner sense of possibility, you are able to move forward toward your highest goals and self-realization. Be courageous in your momentum.

Evening Reflection: My Insights from Today

January 18, _____

Mental
Watch the stories you tell yourself and others.

Spiritual
Balance your body/instinct/mind and feeling/instinct/mind
in terms of what you already know about yourself.

Emotional
Limitation is a matter of perception.

Physical
Use your resources carefully, and make sure you consider
your energetic resources before you commit to any activity.

Integration
Inner clarity takes time to unfold and manifest. At any given time, your multidimensional nature veils the scope of universal truths so it is manageable to your mind and life. Take action only when you are aligned to your deepest values and be cautious but at the same time courageous in your goals. What you want to have happen, happens. Take time to meditate and gain clarity before you act.

Evening Reflection: My Insights from Today

_____

_____

_____

_____

_____

_____

_____

_____

_____

_____

January 19, _____

Mental

Things are not always what they seem on first glance.
Look deeply into things.

Spiritual

Attention to your Inner process enhances you spiritually.

Emotional

Consider what you want to have happen before you make any decisions.

Physical

How you do anything is how you do everything.
Be mindful of your body and how you use it.

Integration

Consolidation and assimilation are two processes that are essential in growth. Both processes balance and unbalance you while you realign and adjust to new ways of perceiving, knowing, and being. Take time to gain clarity internally so you envision your highest goals and align to your true divine nature. Live your life fully and freely. Remember, when you are free being you, you experience your divinity.

Evening Reflection: My Insights from Today

January 20, _____

Mental
Your inner dialogue is important in orienting your thinking.
Be mindful of the stories you tell yourself.
Watch for limiting beliefs and limiting ways of thinking.

Spiritual
Take time to meditate in your own private space.

Emotional
Consider how your emotions impact others. Think before you act.

Physical
You may find yourself prone to overeating today.
Be mindful and disciplined.

Integration
Your inner direction is often influenced by those around you, unless you are clear about what you want to have happen, and resonates deeply with your inner core. Stay in a loving place, and from that space, limit your focus so you determine what is right for you and how you want to proceed to create whatever you want to have happen. It is your choice to stay in the flow or move away from it. Be true to your inner Self and take time to be alone to gain clarity.

Evening Reflection: My Insights from Today

January 21, _____

Mental
Behaving based on the needs of others
distracts you from your inner process.

Spiritual
Intuition is best heard when you take time
to focus and listen to the quiet voice within.

Emotional
Anxiety and fear of rejection may trigger emotional reactivity
and result in precipitous actions.

Physical
Overexertion from pushing your body too much is a danger.

Integration
When you are distracted, what kind of distraction is your distraction? And
when distracted, is there a relationship between distraction and moving
forward in your life? Listen for the inner voice of your higher Self and trust
that you know more than you think you know. By limiting your attention
and focus, you can move toward your inner purpose with direction and
confidence.

Evening Reflection: My Insights from Today

January 22, _____

Mental
Watch your thoughts. Keep them positive.

Spiritual
Self-recognition is key to feeling inner strength and empowerment.
You know more than you think you know.

Emotional
Watch your words carefully,
especially when what others do surprises you.

Physical
Be sure to get plenty of "down time"
so you can replenish your physical reserves.

Integration
Your individual path is most exciting when you allow yourself to imagine the unimaginable. Consider what you already know and identify it. From this space of imagining, what possibilities might open up for you? Is there anything you now know about your situation/path? How can your path be better than this? Dream and imagine, and stay with your inner process.

Evening Reflection: My Insights from Today

January 23, _____

Mental
You may find yourself on mental overload.
Be patient and consider all facets of an idea,
and be careful about hidden assumptions and judgments.

Spiritual
Patterns and experiences with a common thread
connect you to your deepest Self. Pay attention.

Emotional
Shift internally when you experience any disharmonious reactions.
Release the feeling and reassess your inner space.

Physical
Your body is always sensitive to outside elements.
Be alert to your body's needs and
take care of them lovingly and patiently.

Integration
While taking a few moments to tune in to your inner voice, consider what
you know about the risks your imaginings carry? What do you want to have
happen? And when it happens, what happens in your body? Are you aligned
to expect the unexpected? Do you confront it within your imaginings? Do you
stay centered in your inner wisdom and knowing? Find your center and live
from there.

Evening Reflection: My Insights from Today

January 24, _____

Mental
Self-empowerment comes through waiting for mental clarity.

Spiritual
Alertness for your inner voice brings you closer to your inner awareness.

Emotional
Pay attention to details to which you automatically react.
These details point you toward adjustments
that can bring you into alignment.

Physical
Good health is linked to self-awareness of body responses.

Integration
The mind codes and processes information faster than you can comprehend. Because of how your mind works, it is impossible to know the roots of any image, so it is important to always ask the simple questions, "What do I know about this now?" and "Is there anything else I know now?" These two questions can allow you to delve into your own inner knowing in ways that can unearth patterns and expectations beneath your awareness. Be courageous and seek to know what you already know. Ask these questions throughout your day.

Evening Reflection: My Insights from Today

January 25, _____

Mental

When you open your mind to new ways of thinking, you open yourself to new options you may have never envisioned for yourself. Be courageous.

Spiritual

Change yourself to change your life. Listen to the depth of your inner Self.

Emotional

Emotional options for behavior are best rehearsed prior to action. Be still.

Physical

Your body gives you subtle cues through your senses. Use all your senses.

Integration

When remembering past situations, what would you have wished would have happened? Take special care of your body in ways that pamper it and you. And when inside your body, what kind of feelings are the feelings of knowing what you know? Be mindful and write down what you are grateful for in your body and the tangible reasons for it.

Evening Reflection: My Insights from Today

January 26, _____

Mental
Discipline yourself to register smells and tastes and notice them.

Spiritual
Meditate in your own space today. Take quiet time alone.

Emotional
Emotions may run high so monitor them.

Physical
Chemistry speaks a language your cells understand.
Listen to them.

Integration
What kinds of opportunities present themselves to you now? What do you know about what is important to you now? When you take quiet time, consider how you might focus in on your inner process by asking probing self-reflective questions that deepen your inner knowledge by opening you to new opportunities. Visualize the impossible and consider them possible.

Evening Reflection: My Insights from Today

January 27, _____

Mental
All areas of life can be considered and their balance realigned.

Spiritual
Find a way to align your desires with your spiritual goals.

Emotional
You are the master of your fate. Take charge of your emotions.

Physical
Immune health depends on subtle input.
Recognize the strength of your body, and build on that.

Integration
You live in multidimensional consciousness although you are often only aware of your conscious functioning. Ask questions that deepen your knowledge and understanding of the generally invisible worlds. What do you now know about the four ways of being, i.e., the Four Worlds? And when you balance yourself, what kind of balance is that balance? Use the day to gain inner awareness — it is a wise use of your time.

Evening Reflection: My Insights from Today

January 28, _____

Mental
Watch the interplay between your mind and your intuition today.

Spiritual
Trust intuitive knowing that whispers to you.

Emotional
How you connect with others
in different situations tells you a great deal.

Physical
Push your body only in ways that enhance your overall health.

Integration
When you expand into your deepest Self, what do you know about yourself?
When you retreat more deeply into yourself, is there anything else you know
now? From this deep place, what would you like to have happen? These questions are key questions that have the capacity to shift awareness so you can
align to all parts of yourself.

Evening Reflection: My Insights from Today

January 29, _____

Mental

What happens internally for you when you focus your mind?
What would you like to have happen?

Spiritual

When you use your internal watchful awareness to inform your choices,
you are likely to be more aligned with yourself.

Emotional

Unique, shifting, and innovative energies change how you feel.

Physical

Cells change, so bring attention to them for awareness.

Integration

Listen to your emotions, and as you listen to them, notice, just notice, what
you know about the circumstances and situations you are in. Discern fact
from desire. In consciousness, discernment and recognizing what you want
to have happen may or may not align with what is possible to have happen.
Your state of being is important. Pay attention.

Evening Reflection: My Insights from Today

January 30, _____

Mental

Consider the consequences of your possible thoughts, words,
and actions prior to implementing any of them.

Spiritual

Your sensitivity to others can override your inner sensitivities.
Be generous to yourself by taking the time you need for yourself.

Emotional

Use emotional strength to reorient and keep your moods in perspective.

Physical

Build your immune health. Exercise with caution.

Integration

Those around you influence your experiences and may even affect your
judgment. Be mindfully aware of yourself in relationship to others and pay
special attention to what happened just before you felt what you felt. From
this place and space here, what would you now like to have happen? And
what do you imagine will happen inside of you when this occurs?

Evening Reflection: My Insights from Today

January 31, _____

Mental
Pressure from too much input may confuse you.

Spiritual
Consider yourself as a sensitive instrument that is best when it is in tune.

Emotional
Emotions continue to run high so react to others in measured ways.

Physical
Exercise with extreme caution and eat carefully when with others.

Integration
As you receive information in the now, you have an opportunity to recreate reality for yourself. Use this time to refine and heal your past by allowing new possibilities to surface, and use your senses to align all layers of consciousness. Remember your feelings and processes of the past few days and weeks. What happened just before you were most aligned? And what else is possible?

Evening Reflection: My Insights from Today

February 1, _____

Mental

Pay attention to your inner alignment and frame past experiences
so you find new ways to handle situations that move you toward your goals.

Spiritual

Pay attention to your doubts; "when in doubt, sit it out."

Emotional

Emotional reactivity is high so take your time,
especially around other people.

Physical

Your body has its own way of balancing itself.
Trust it, and watch for dips in energy as indicators that you need rest.

Integration

Emotional sensitivity may influence what you want to have happen in your
current situation. Take time to center yourself in your body and balance the
Axes of Awareness (see resources on page 373). When sensitive and vulnerable, what do you want to have happen next?

Evening Reflection: My Insights from Today

_____

_____

_____

_____

_____

_____

_____

_____

_____

_____

February 2, _____

Mental

Consider new possibilities in what you would like to have happen.

Spiritual

When tuning in to yourself,
what do you know about your deepest goals?

Emotional

Consider your body when you respond emotionally
and check for alignment.

Physical

Promising more than you can deliver puts you
under physical as well as emotional stress.

Integration

Direction of your highest Self is most crucial in aligning and balancing in your life. From your current space, what do you know about your direction now? And when you say "I," whereabouts is your "I"? Is it in your head, your body, or outside? And is there a difference between your inner voice and your emotions?

Evening Reflection: My Insights from Today

February 3, _____

Mental

How you think affects the way you act.
Take in all points of view, and draw upon past experiences in the present.

Spiritual

Deep inner knowing that moves you to action leads to right action.

Emotional

Balancing the *Axes of Awareness* (see resources on page 373)
is essential for your health.

Physical

Take time alone and away from the activities of daily life
to rebalance and refresh your energy.

Integration

Allow for possibilities that may manifest in the near future. Take time to listen to the voices of others. Listen to their concerns and to their optimism as well. Solutions emerge when you think "outside the box," and when you imagine and project images for others as well. Put your concerns on hold when you wait for your Self-Knowing to be secure. What do you want to happen? It is likely to happen if you envision it clearly.

Evening Reflection: My Insights from Today

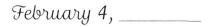

February 4, _____

Mental
Creative thought is especially beneficial
when you apply it to your life and build awareness.

Spiritual
Trust your inner voice and sense of inner balance
more than anything or anyone else.

Emotional
Listen more to your gut than to the opinions of other people.

Physical
Only push your body in ways you know are healthy for you.

Integration
Stay tuned to remembering what you know about your creative passion. It drives your direction and your purpose in life. Ask, "When I'm going in the right direction, that's like what?" and, "Am I going in the right direction for myself now?" Your future is set in motion now. If you are going in the right direction now, you are likely to find that what you want to have happen is likely to manifest. Stay focused and on track.

Evening Reflection: My Insights from Today

February 5, _____

Mental
With lots of information coming in from many arenas,
it is wise to keep focused on what is important.

Spiritual
Creative energy depends on your ability to self-reflect
and tap into your inner core.

Emotional
When your feelings come from deep within you in a balanced way,
you are likely to know more than you recognize.
At such times, call upon your subtle perceptions for confirmation.

Physical
Eat with discipline and only what you know is healthy for you.
Avoid overindulging.

Integration
What you know or think you know may shift as you shift your focus and
awareness. When you are alone, what do you know about how what you know
guides your integrated wisdom? And what kind of wisdom is your wisdom?
What do you want to have happen from this place/space here?

Evening Reflection: My Insights from Today

_____

_____

_____

_____

_____

_____

_____

_____

February 6, _____

Mental
What you think affects others as well as yourself.
Use your mind with intention and awareness of consequences.

Spiritual
When you meditate, you tap the depth of your inner Self
and find connections that help guide your life.

Emotional
Notice feelings, but rely on your past experiences and intuition more than
on your reactions to what is happening around you in the moment.

Physical
Be cautious about overdoing things that deplete your energy.

Integration
What difference do you recognize between what you perceive and what you
feel? And from that space there, what do you want to have happen? This question is key in gaining clarity to manifest your future congruently for yourself
and your life. Take time to self-reflect. Your intuition empowers you. Listen to
your intuitive voice and take action only if you know it deeply resonates with
your higher Self.

Evening Reflection: My Insights from Today

February 7, _____

Mental

You are often judged by the perception of others
rather than by what you intend.
Consider how other people perceive what you communicate.

Spiritual

It is essential to revisit issues and take note
of how you have changed with time.

Emotional

Stay positive and open to all possibilities
without committing to any one path.

Physical

Knowing when to push your body and
when to rest is essential to your health.

Integration

Recognize how your body informs you about patterns and cycles that enhance your life and wellbeing, especially emotionally. Notice, just notice, how each step along your life experiences to this point in time have emerged from your best efforts in terms of your awareness at that time. Empower your inner Self. Ask, "And from this space here, what do I know now?" Encourage all who touch your life in positive ways so they can attain more. Take time to be self-reflective. Awareness is a process.

Evening Reflection: My Insights from Today

_____

_____

_____

_____

_____

_____

_____

_____

February 8, _____

Mental
Avoid taking action in response to outside pressures.

Spiritual
When intuition guides your choices, and you recognize patterns
that worked for you in the past. Trust yourself.

Emotional
Align in your life to what you know with certainty
and relate only to supportive people.

Physical
Care for yourself with self-discipline and awareness.

Integration
New insight about instinctive perceptions, as they relate to what activates
through your senses, take on new meaning for you. Ask, "When I recognize
what is beneath the surface of awareness, that's like what?" Learn from your
insights about yourself to break down illusions that may be standing in your
way of manifesting your highest dreams and goals. And when illusions are
out of the way, what do you want to have happen next? What else is possible?

Evening Reflection: My Insights from Today

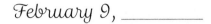

February 9, _____

Mental

Observe your mind at work but wait to draw any conclusions.

Spiritual

Take time alone to meditate. Pay attention to your breathing,
and breathe as if the Divine is breathing you. Be still in your breathing
and make it so quiet that you disappear into the breath.

Emotional

Self-awareness is key before you commit yourself to any particular path.

Physical

Be wary about depleting your energetic resources,
and pay attention to what your body tells you.

Integration

The mind is a very important center of awareness that discerns truth from desires based on factual reality in the now. Use this knowing of what you are vulnerable to as a way to recognize your tendency toward emotional reactivity. Gain clarity without judgment of good/bad, right/wrong. What do you know now? What is possible based on fact rather than desire? And have you considered all perspectives about what you want to have happen from this place here, now? Remember: The future is now, know it, change it.

Evening Reflection: My Insights from Today

February 10, _____

Mental

Sensitivity to how you are perceived may activate you emotionally.
Be mindful about where and how you spend time.

Spiritual

Stay focused on your inner path, despite outside pressures.

Emotional

Depth of understanding and awareness of yourself is key to emotional
balance. Use your creative intelligence when challenged by the day.

Physical

Protect your immune system by staying close to home.

Integration

When moving forward in your life, what kinds of challenges are in the way?
What kinds of commitments are the commitments you make to yourself?
When you plan with a vision to move forward in your life, what do you want
to have happen next? Use your past experiences to inform the present by
recalling what worked in the past, and call upon others who met similar
challenges in ways you value.

Evening Reflection: My Insights from Today

_____

_____

_____

_____

_____

_____

_____

_____

_____

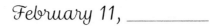

February 11, _____

Mental
Consider the principles that guide your life.
Align your thinking and emotions to honor them
in others as well as in yourself.

Spiritual
Visualize how you can best advance your inner purpose and pay attention.

Emotional
Emotional reactions tell you the impact of people
and situations on your health.

Physical
Body and feeling reactions tell you what your body wants you to hear.

Integration
When you know how to move forward, what kind of knowing is that knowing?
What difference is there between what you know and what you feel? How do
you know the difference? Whereabouts is that difference, inside or outside?
Take in information, and find a space that feels right. From this space, what
do you know now? And from this space here, now, what is possible? What
else is possible?

Evening Reflection: My Insights from Today

February 12, _____

Mental
Make use of this time to note concretely what affects your life,
but stay open to changing your perceptions.

Spiritual
Aligning to your multidimensional nature
is key to living in the flow of your highest Self.

Emotional
When you recognize emotional energy in yourself,
take some moments to tune in to it, and consider
what you want to have happen before you react.

Physical
Be open to all input from your body, and work toward aligning
your physical structure as well as your body chemistry.

Integration
Inner transformation depends on accessing emotional vulnerabilities that
you can release energetically. Revisit stories you tell yourself or were told by
those close to you about yourself and your life. Retell these stories by asking
yourself *Clean Questions* (see resources on page 373) so your future has a
new path to forge for you. Pay special attention to how you are different when
with others and when by yourself. What do you know now?

Evening Reflection: My Insights from Today

Mental

It is wise to ask many questions today prior to forming opinions.
Be cautious using words. Once spoken, words have form and energy.

Spiritual

Recognize your vulnerability to the sensitivities of others.

Emotional

Use your senses to monitor your feelings.
Go to the depth of what you feel and call upon past experiences.

Physical

Eat and exercise very carefully and slowly.

Integration

Emotions color perspective and carry a thread of desire for you into the
future. Notice the way you shift energetically when other people are around.
From this place of clarity and recognition, form a vision of what you want to
have happen as you continue to relate to others in the world in your daily life.
Set your resolve to stay aligned to your inner process by giving permission to
your higher Self and what you know from that space to inform you what is of
highest service to your divine Self. Love what you do and do what you love.
Stay aware of your balance within.

Evening Reflection: My Insights from Today

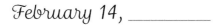

February 14, _____

Mental

Pressures from others may push you toward premature action.
Stay true to yourself and your inner wisdom.

Spiritual

Take quiet time alone so you can rebalance
and listen to your inner voice rather than to energy of others.

Emotional

Use your inner depth to monitor how you interpret emotions.
Be wary of emotional reactivity.

Physical

Physical signals tell you how you really feel about
people, places, and things.

Integration

Before you speak, pay attention to the energy behind your thoughts, words, and contemplated deeds. When you are emotionally open, words spoken by you or those around you carry great impact and feed your unconscious with images and messages that resonate within your cells. When speaking, it is essential that you consider what you want to have happen and what impact you might have on the other person. Staying true to your highest values is key in all interactive relationships, including those with yourself.

Evening Reflection: My Insights from Today

February 15, _____

Mental
Play with information and images before thinking about things concretely.

Spiritual
Breathing informs you of how you perceive external conditions,
so listen with all your senses.

Emotional
Emotions may run strong so watch your reactions and monitor them.
Watch your words.

Physical
You may tend toward overindulgence when in social situations.
Be mindful.

Integration
You are an instrument of great sensitivity, and as such, your task is to recognize when you are in tune or out of tune and need "tuning." Review your capacity to create what you envision in your life. Remain open to information from dreams. When you are asleep, collective archetypes imprint the unconscious you, i.e., you move into a deep connection with the totality, and at that time you are increasingly open to universal rather than to individual energies. At different points in the day, you respond from different layers of consciousness to integrate the way subtle variations in energy affect you in the world. The more time you take to self-reflect on your internal balance, the more congruently you express it outwardly. Be patient and take your time.

Evening Reflection: My Insights from Today

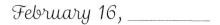

February 16, _____

Mental
When you think about the next steps in your life,
what do you know about the role you want to be in?

Spiritual
When most true to yourself, that's like what?

Emotional
Emotional resilience is the key to balance.
Take time to consider your emotions and their impact before you react.

Physical
You may be inclined to do more than is good for your body.
Take care of your health.

Integration
In every moment of time, you have freedom to realign and create your future.
Ask, "What do I want to have happen from this space here?" Pay attention
to your remembrances from past similar situations and feelings and ask,
"From this place here, now, what do I want to have happen?" As you remain
open to new ideas and you move from your current awareness and goals, you
create a new future filled with possibilities. Consider, "What else is possible?"

Evening Reflection: My Insights from Today

Mental

Overload and stress may surprise you unless you
set your intention to listen carefully for your inner voice and
stay away from any emotional arguments.

Spiritual

Your intuition tells you when you are in situations that carry stress for you.
Ask, "Am I going in the right direction? Am I in the right space for myself?"

Emotional

Take time to consider consequences of emotional reactions
before you speak or act.

Physical

Pushing your body may compromise your health.

Integration

Taking action from a space of clarity brings success. Action from a space
of fogginess is likely to challenge you in the future. Recognize that what you
intend manifests in exactly the way your unconscious frames it, whether
clear or cloudy. Remain patient with complexities of feelings that take time
for you to grasp on both the spiritual and on the emotional layers of your
awareness. Often, it happens that events begin to take form much before
you experience them in your life; in addition, events unfold over time, often
taking three months for closure to take root. Give yourself this time to allow
your process to emerge and to fully register in consciousness. Today, and in
general right now, you are likely to feel sensitive and vulnerable to the desires
of others. Second guessing yourself is to be expected; trust your inner knowing. Rely on past self-awareness to carry you through this time.

Evening Reflection: My Insights from Today

_____

_____

_____

_____

_____

Mental

Think things through deeply and carefully
so you assure right action in the long run.

Spiritual

When you take charge of your destiny and use your
creative intelligence, you are more likely to make choices that
you feel align at all layers of yourself.

Emotional

Avoid provoking others by acting at cross-purposes with them.

Physical

Exercise and eat with self-discipline
but with love of your body and its strength.

Integration

Visualize projects you want to fulfill in the next three months. Keep in mind
the image of "what you want to have happen" and use this as a mantra
when you lose focus. At times in the near future, you might wonder why you
thought you could accomplish the things you visualized. Remember, keep
true to your Self-purpose. It is what you know and no one else can know. At
the same time, open to creative input of others who share what has "worked
for them." Learn from the experiences of others as well as from your own
experiences. We are finishing a visionary period and moving into the time
when receptivity to feelings of others and to their grasp of your ideas may
help advance your desires. Use this information to build your highest potential as a conscious, aware human being.

Evening Reflection: My Insights from Today

February 19, _____

Mental
Before you take any action, take time to visualize what you want to have happen, and consider if the action would move you toward your goals.

Spiritual
Remain sensitive and empathic to others
while keeping your emotions in check.

Emotional
Maintain emotional balance as you transform reactivity through awareness.

Physical
Eat and exercise with awareness of what your body needs.

Integration
When emotions shift in you, are the emotions your emotions or are you responding and reacting to those around you? Take on only those things that you deeply resonate with over time, and pay careful attention to how you use your resources, both inner and outer. You are a powerful vehicle for manifesting your desires. What do you want to have happen at this time, from this space? Are you in the "right" perspective? And how far are you from your goal? These questions can be used as a self-reflective guide. Pay attention. Act only when clear.

Evening Reflection: My Insights from Today

_____

_____

_____

_____

_____

_____

_____

_____

February 20, _____

Mental

Your mind is a powerful tool that can work for your benefit or against you.
Be mindful of how you talk to yourself and what pressures you put on yourself.

Spiritual

Envision your path before you make any commitments
to assure inner certainty.

Emotional

You are open to the emotions of others. Be alert for what
you want to commit to, and err on the side of less rather than more.

Physical

Use caution in exercise and monitor your eating while stressed.

Integration

The balance between what you think and what you feel may need realignment.
Because you are a biological being, there are always chemical influences on
you that are out of your conscious control. Use your body and its signaling
systems as a tool for awareness. Pay attention to your internal and external
resources and how you use them. Take time to self-reflect with the key question: "And, what do I know now?" This one question can change your life if
you use it throughout your day. Download *Transformational Synthesis* (see
resources on page 373), listen to it and use it to learn to balance meditatively
while aware of your body.

Evening Reflection: My Insights from Today

February 21, _____

Mental

Try out new possibilities before settling on what you think you might do.
Consider the question: "And what do I know about this action now?"
Ask yourself this question six times.

Spiritual

You become a beacon of light for others when you honor
your inner process and stay true to your highest Self.

Emotional

You are highly sensitive and vulnerable to others.
Be clear with yourself and honor yourself as much as you do others.

Physical

Continue caution in any physical overindulgence.

Integration

Hold gently but firmly to the images of possibilities for the future that you
envision for yourself. By holding inner connections firmly in your mind you
give them importance and allow future possibilities to affirm what direction
they want to move toward. Tension within comes from the inner impera-
tive to find balance between body/instinct/mind and feelings/instinct/mind.
Understanding this need for balance and how it works is critical in self-
awareness. What is the balance between what you know and what you feel?

Evening Reflection: My Insights from Today

February 22, _____

Mental

How you think about your options in taking action is important.
Think in positive terms and listen for your inner voice for guidance.

Spiritual

Promises put undue pressure on you
to act at a time best spent meditatively.

Emotional

Avoid interacting with anyone who evokes negative feelings
in you about yourself.

Physical

Use your energy wisely, and make sure you rest when you feel at all tired.

Integration

Focus on your strengths, i.e., your skills in the world, more than on the things
you want to have manifest. Be wary of overextending yourself to others. Make
certain that you follow and plan for what you want to have happen, and direct
your focused attention to achieve your goals. You may create confusion, for
yourself, and others, if you act based on information that misaligns to your
deepest Self. Take time alone so you tune in to your deepest sense of inner
calm and stay focused despite outside pressures. Always ask, "What do I
want to have happen now?" and "What else is possible?"

Evening Reflection: My Insights from Today

_____

_____

_____

_____

_____

_____

_____

February 23, _____

Mental
Re-evaluate your relationships in terms of how they
support you in reaching your goals.

Spiritual
Remain focused on your strengths,
and consider how you can expand your talents.

Emotional
Feel the effect of others on the way you feel about yourself.

Physical
Stay quiet until you have focus and balance
that comes from a quiet place inside you.

Integration
Give priority to awareness rather than action today. Focus on your strengths,
i.e., your skills in the world more than on what you want to manifest. Center
and wait for inner knowing before deciding what actions might be "right
action." Because you are likely to shift perspective over time, take this opportunity to gain clarity about your inner process so when you take action, you
act from your deepest Self. What do you know about yourself now?

Evening Reflection: My Insights from Today

_____

_____

_____

_____

_____

_____

_____

_____

February 24, _____

Mental
You could be on information overload today, so avoid overstimulation.

Spiritual
The inner voice is your best guide today, so wait for it to whisper to you.

Emotional
Pay attention to the way the needs of others fit with your known needs.

Physical
You are sensitive and vulnerable to energy around you today.
Be attentive to your body and to yourself.

Integration
Manifestation expresses the deep inner Self spiritually. Misusing your energy by spending it foolishly or in ways that dissipate it depletes inner balance and purpose. Pay attention to those who enhance your life while moving back from those who deplete you. In this way, you conserve your life force and set up patterns for future amplification that bring life enhancing health. This is a time to build your strength and your resources. What you feel today had its roots in the fall. Pay attention to how you feel so you can utilize awareness from these past three months to piece together insights and use your insights in your life. The more aware you remain to your cycles of emotion as they relate to those around you now, the more comfortable you will feel in the spring. All possibilities regularly flow into us through new combinations of energy configurations reminiscent of the past. When you remember the past, you can reframe the present. Thus, you create the future. Take dominion over your personality and remain optimistic.

Evening Reflection: My Insights from Today

February 25, _____

Mental
You could be on information overload
with more questions than answers. Avoid overstimulation.

Spiritual
You live in Four Worlds. Meditation time aligns these worlds internally
and allows you to balance them with awareness.
Take time to listen to your inner voice and align energetically.

Emotional
Consider the impact of others on your feelings and how they push you.

Physical
Eat very cautiously and with discipline, especially in social situations.

Integration
Often, feelings beneath the surface of awareness drive actions in challenging ways. Pay special attention to how you create reality. Any area where you frame words in ways that might compromise your true intent, even by slightly distorting its strength or perspective, give your unconscious permission to manifest in subtly misaligned ways. Honesty requires courage. Courage requires you to be strong enough to face disapproval from others, while standing up lovingly for yourself. What do you want to have happen?

Evening Reflection: My Insights from Today

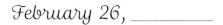

February 26, _____

Mental

Remain open-minded when considering the way things
and people affect you. Consider reframing your stories.

Spiritual

Stay with what you know works for you, and stay quiet when possible.

Emotional

Remember past interactions with those in your life, and use that information.

Physical

When you know what you feel, what happens in your body?

Integration

Feelings under the surface of awareness are likely to trip you up unless you
stay focused and use your skills to project what you want to have happen in
the future. Be careful when with other people who are emotionally reactive,
and ask yourself if you are in the right perspective and facing in the right
direction. Balance your body/instinct/mind and your feelings/instinct/mind
by taking time for meditation and self-reflection. Take dominion of your personality by recognizing and aspiring to your highest goal in each situation
and staying true to it.

Evening Reflection: My Insights from Today

February 27, _____

Mental
Imagine how contemplated action may impact you in the future,
before you commit to it.

Spiritual
Notice how you are with different people and different situations.
Meditate on what aligns with you, and how you can
use this knowledge to gain awareness.

Emotional
Pay attention to the way others support your life purpose
as you see it unfolding.

Physical
Avoid overexertion and overeating. Make sure you rest when you are tired.

Integration
When you recognize the limitations of your inner and outer resources, where
is your focus? Being aware of the way you talk to yourself and how you frame
what limits you is key in moving forward toward aligning yourself at all levels
of being. You exist simultaneously in multiple dimensions. Move outside your
ordinary thinking and consider what else is possible.

Evening Reflection: My Insights from Today

February 28, _____

Mental

Tension between what you think and what others think may challenge you.

Spiritual

Balance between what you know you want to have happen
and what you feel should happen may need consideration.
Take time to gain insight and listen to your inner Self.

Emotional

Recognize that tides of emotions have times of calm and times of turbulence.
Wait for inner balance before reacting.

Physical

Make sure all areas of your life support your health.

Integration

Frustration may surface for you when you grope for understanding and
attempt to express yourself. Call upon metaphoric stories to explain your
point rather than seeking to describe or elaborate through your own words.
Stories that come to mind probably have relevance to the feelings beneath
your consciousness. Use this component of the day's planetary movements
to connect to another facet of your mind. Watch how clearly you can make
connections when you retrieve stories, even movies, that bring associations
to the forefront of your mind. Look at the storylines for cues that can resolve
some mysteries of your life. As your life unfolds, patterns behind the veil of
appearances begin to form pictures moving into motion carrying you forward. Follow each tributary before you make decisions.

Evening Reflection: My Insights from Today

_____

_____

_____

_____

_____

Mental
Information overload may confuse you, so avoid major mental decisions.

Spiritual
Intuition is especially helpful today in guiding your direction.

Emotional
Emotional reactivity may conflict with what is healthiest for you.

Physical
Make sure all areas of your life support your health.

Integration
You may feel driven toward action today, and if you feel certain that your considered action is founded on a strong sense that such action will honor what you want and feel will serve you, take action. If, however, you sense any doubts or misgivings, wait and reconsider in a few days. The day brings strong energy that you can use to gain momentum or you can wait for calmer days and less pressure coming from outside. You are in the driver's seat here. Do not act unless such action comes from within you without pressure from others.

Evening Reflection: My Insights from Today

_____

_____

_____

_____

_____

_____

_____

_____

_____

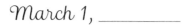

March 1, _____

Mental

Self-talk gives you a wealth of information about your self-presentation. What do you want to have happen? Keep this question in mind.

Spiritual

Your openness and vulnerability to the needs of others
may create confusion for you.

Emotional

Pressures from others may cause emotional reactivity in you.

Physical

Make sure you plan your meals and eat according to your body's needs.

Integration

Balancing body/instinct/mind and feelings/instinct/mind is a challenge when different situations and people activate different responses for you. What do you know about what aligns you when pulled in different directions between what you know and what you feel? Smells may bring remembrances that can align you. If you have an essential oil or some other smell that you love, use it to remember how you experience inner alignment when in an empowered sense of Self. Use your mind to discern what is important. Stay true to yourself.

Evening Reflection: My Insights from Today

March 2, _____

Mental
Questioning past assumptions
and raising new questions can serve you well.

Spiritual
Watching internal shifts shows what deeply resonates with you
at a deep level of yourself.

Emotional
Past events in your life can motivate you to embrace new ideas
when framed in new ways.

Physical
Dissonance between the messages from your body
and the messages from your mind may confuse you.
Err on the side of less rather than more today.

Integration
Focus on how your mental orientation affects your feelings. Just notice how your words affect others. Be mindful of how much more you second-guess yourself emotionally when you are alone than when in the presence of others. During this time you may find that your animals lend great comfort. They often have the capacity to bring energetic connections that otherwise occur only when you sleep. Use your inner sense of what you know has resonated with you in the past to anchor yourself. Envision what you desire in order to begin anew a process of manifestation for the future. What do you want to have happen?

Evening Reflection: My Insights from Today

_____

_____

_____

_____

_____

March 3, _____

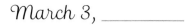

Mental

Ask if your proposed actions are congruent with how you want to be perceived and what you want to have happen for yourself in your life.

Spiritual

Focus in meditation today on *Empowered Self-talk* (see resources on page 373), so you bring empowered energy into your body.

Emotional

Balance body/instinct/mind and feeling/instinct/mind *Axes of Awareness* (see resources on page 373).

Physical

Use anxieties to monitor your body and emotional balance.

Integration

So much of your self-concept derives from the experience of how people and events have come together for you in the past. Look, especially now, toward new perspectives for using yourself in the world. It is a time when innovative ideas have the potential to take root within you in order to form new patterns in the future. Think about the people with whom you associate. Do you enjoy their company? Do they enhance your sense of ease and confidence in the world? Do you feel healthy when you are in their presence? Feelings, as well as what you conceptualize about the world, are especially affected by others now. Thus, take this opportunity to gain support through new communications with others through your mindfulness regarding their affect on you. Keep quieter than you might feel in order to conserve your energy. Eat very carefully.

Evening Reflection: My Insights from Today

March 4, _____

Mental

Consider new possibilities that may open the door
to new ways of perceiving yourself.

Spiritual

Listen to your instincts and follow what feels right for you.
Take time to meditate.

Emotional

The depth of what you feel may surprise you.
Keep your emotions in balance and avoid impulsive reactivity.

Physical

Eat with awareness rather than for comfort.

Integration

Take time to allow contemplation of what responses belong to you vs. those
that belong to the collective consciousness with which you connect spiritually. Instincts in the presence of others and when you sleep influence your
inner core. If you doubt your feelings and instincts, take time to be clear
before taking any action. Remember how important breath is for balance.
No one on this planet survives without sufficient oxygen; you receive oxygen
through breathing. Pay attention to how you take this essential resource into
your body. Use inhalation and exhalation of air as a model of the ebb and flow
of energy in your day-to-day life. Breathe as though the Divine breathes you.

Evening Reflection: My Insights from Today

March 5, _____

Mental
Pay attention to innovative ways you can re-craft the image of your life.

Spiritual
Remain fairly internal in your process despite feeling pressures to manifest.

Emotional
Stay with your desires rather than giving in to those of others.

Physical
Health requires quiet rest balanced with activity.
Make sure your day includes both.

Integration
Doubts are natural in the process of reconciling opposites and in gaining clarity. When you use inner doubt as a way to question your assumptions, you have the potential to reach truth. Remain open to shifting your perspective while you consider alternatives to your thinking. Ask, "What if _____?" Take your time to recognize familiar patterns in yourself and others, and take this opportunity to gather new information that may inform your decisions.

Evening Reflection: My Insights from Today

March 6, _____

Mental
When listening to your inner Self, what do you know
about yourself and what is important to you?

Spiritual
Envisioning your future sets your intention in consciousness.

Emotional
Be cautious about emotional responses by considering
what aligns with your highest Self.

Physical
When you pay attention to your breathing,
you are better able to monitor your stress.

Integration
What kind of dominion do you have over your feelings? Personality challenges can be used to bring out your highest values and highest aspirations of Self. What do you know about your highest Self? When you are aligned congruently to your true Self, what kind of alignment is that alignment? And that alignment is like what? From this space here, what do you know now?

Evening Reflection: My Insights from Today

_____

_____

_____

_____

_____

_____

_____

_____

_____

_____

_____

_____

March 7, _____

Mental
Action that honors what you know about yourself
and your inner resources is action well spent.

Spiritual
Reflect on times you took inner authority that triggered other people.

Emotional
How you react to others is how you react to yourself.

Physical
You are likely to physically overextend yourself if you succumb
to outside pressures. Be protective of your health.

Integration
What and how you think is important in how you feel and what happens in
setting and reaching your goals. Before you take any action, it is important
that you make sure you are in the "right" space, and facing in the "right"
direction. Consider all possibilities for your future before you determine
how you want to move forward. You can tune in to your senses and to how
you experience the impact of others on you, if you take the time to do so.
Remember that energy follows thought. If you do not already do so, it is a
good time to begin writing down what you are grateful for, adding "because I
_____," to the gratitude statement.

Evening Reflection: My Insights from Today

March 8, _____

Mental
Avoid mental pressure to do things that could stress you physically today.

Spiritual
You are sensitive and empathic to others and to the collective.
Take extra time to meditate so you can balance yourself energetically.

Emotional
Be honest about what you want to do,
and limit your commitments accordingly.

Physical
Stay with your health program despite pressures from others.

Integration
All contemplated actions use your inner resources. At the same time, connection and feedback from your body inform you toward action so you protect yourself and your loved ones. When you experience daily pressures, always ask, "Am I in the "right" place, am I facing in the "right" direction?" The pressures on you now require diligence in recognizing your perspective. Make time in your day to regularly assess your positioning.

Evening Reflection: My Insights from Today

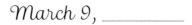

March 9, _____

Mental
Overload and overthinking before the time is ripe leads to stress.

Spiritual
Remain open to all possibilities within yourself to allow time its process.

Emotional
Conserve emotional energy
while protecting all your inner and outer resources.

Physical
Avoid exercise and overindulgences to enhance your health.

Integration
Mental pressure may raise questions that create confusion about how to proceed in relationships or in social situations. Instead of struggling with any decisions on a day when you are unlikely to resolve things adequately, simply relax about things and wait for a more advantageous day for such pursuits. Strong energy that drives you from your will often leads to disappointments later. Stay close to home. Stay conservative in your eating and spending. Conservation is important in all areas.

Evening Reflection: My Insights from Today

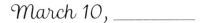

March 10, _____

Mental
Mental pressures may cause you to feel stress
about where you want to be and what you want to do.

Spiritual
Taking time for your inner process
is essential in staying on track in your life.

Emotional
How you take care of yourself is as crucial as how you care for others.
Take responsibility for yourself.

Physical
Your "nose" knows. Pay attention to what it tells you.

Integration
Internal dissonance between your body, instincts, feelings, and mind may create confusion as you attempt to find what resonates deeply when balancing your needs with those of others and of the environment. As you make decisions about anything today, make certain that you remain cognizant of your inner limitations in terms of how you allocate resources, both internal and external. Who you are with affects your self-esteem. If you use the day's information in this regard, you can benefit greatly in the long run. However, take great care in any decision-making. It is best that you wait before settling on any path that you may later come to regret.

Evening Reflection: My Insights from Today

_____

_____

_____

_____

_____

_____

_____

March 11, _____

Mental
Creative questioning of your process
builds a strong foundation for the future.

Spiritual
When aligned with your highest Self, that's like what?

Emotional
When reacting emotionally, what would you like to have happen?

Physical
Use your senses for information about what resonates with you.

Integration
Pay attention to new sensations, especially those elicited by the sense of smell
and by "feeling" in your body when you enter a room with others or come
into the presence of others. Register information rather than initiating any
action. Inwardly ask questions that need possible answers. You have a chance
to learn how you can reorient in new ways when you think outside your usual
framework and patiently try things on internally before living them out in
reality. You probably try clothes on before you buy them. Do the same with
your anticipated responses. "Try on" responses before you make any decisions about "owning" your interactions. What kind of living is "conscious"
living? And when you are mindful, what do you know about mindfulness?

Evening Reflection: My Insights from Today

March 12, _____

Mental

Use mental discipline to monitor your actions. Breathing is a "tell" about stress and can inform your actions when used consciously.

Spiritual

Meditate with the intention of recognizing your intentions and listen for your inner voice that guides you with love.

Emotional

Keep your emotions in check carefully so they express caring, rather than impatience.

Physical

Stay quiet, avoiding overindulgences of all kinds.

Integration

While you may tell yourself that your emotional reactions serve a "higher purpose," it is in your core Self. Listen for the voice that whispers ever so softly from within and pay attention to what you want to have happen so you have the courage to speak from the knowing part of yourself. Act only when you are clear and centered.

Evening Reflection: My Insights from Today

_____

_____

_____

_____

_____

_____

_____

_____

_____

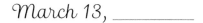

March 13, _____

Mental
Allow yourself to listen to what your body tells you.
Use past experiences and positive self-talk to remain balanced,
even when circumstances around you seem stressful.

Spiritual
Build awareness of connections to others
without losing your perspective.

Emotional
Emotional reactivity lets you know how much pressure you feel.

Physical
Health is related to the effect of others and the environment on you.

Integration
When you connect past experiences to what you want to have happen in the future, what does your self-talk say to you? Observing how you are when with others compared to how you are when alone is important in gaining clarity in terms of inner direction. Find your aligned inner space before you interact with other people. From this space inside, what do you know you want to have happen? Have courage to stay true to yourself.

Evening Reflection: My Insights from Today

March 14, _____

Mental
Stay alert to how you are perceived vs. how you imagine you are perceived.

Spiritual
Stay connected to your inner voice and listen to it carefully for guidance.

Emotional
Pay attention to how communication affects you in social settings.
Avoid taking charge. Commit only to things you are certain you want to do.

Physical
Exercise with care to avoid injury and eat cautiously when out socially.

Integration
Emotional awareness to inner reactions inform where and how you can shift consciousness. Whereabouts is your focus when you speak? Is focus inside or outside? And what do you want to have happen next? These questions are important in identifying where you are in your cyclic process and may be useful in forming goals for your heightened awareness. Use them throughout your day.

Evening Reflection: My Insights from Today

March 15, _____
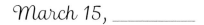

Mental
Use creative intelligence to scan all possibilities before you come
to conclusions. Keep your thinking congruent with your deepest Self.

Spiritual
Align to your deep Self, and pay attention in meditation to your inner voice.
Allow your intuition to guide you.

Emotional
Social intelligence enhances yourself-esteem.
Speak only when you recognize the power of words
and its impact on you and others.

Physical
Be certain to balance body/instinct/mind
and feeling/instinct/mind for health.

Integration
As you move through your day, consider where you are in the cycle of your
emotional reactions and watch your "tells." Note the reactions of others and
how they influence you. What kinds of reactions do you have in reaction to
the reactions of others? What repeating patterns trigger your inner vulnerabilities and what do you know about them now? What do you know about
yourself now?

Evening Reflection: My Insights from Today

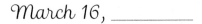

Mental

Take time to recognize positive accomplishments you've made
and how much closer you are in reaching your goals.

Spiritual

Awareness allows light to shine inward, bringing clarity to confusion.
Use all your senses as building blocks to awareness.

Emotional

Vulnerabilities to others can compromise what you need for yourself.
Stay true to what you know about yourself and stand firm without reactivity.

Physical

You need rest and time to reorient and recharge your energy.
Take the time.

Integration

Strong compassion for others, their needs, and your desire to connect with
them may predispose you to put your needs aside for them. Thus, stress
may arise from incongruity between how you are perceived and how you
think you desire to be perceived. Use communication gently and honestly to
express your perspective and to state clearly what you need and want. Be
clear about the difference between needs and values.

Evening Reflection: My Insights from Today

_____

_____

_____

_____

_____

_____

_____

_____

_____

March 17, _____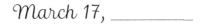

Mental

Pressure from others may influence how you think and what you do.
Take time to reflect on possibilities.

Spiritual

Patience to wait until you know clearly what direction you want to follow
is more important than taking action. Wait for inner knowing.

Emotional

Find a place inside yourself that you recognize
as balanced and without stress.
When in doubt, keep silent and take no action.

Physical

Promising more than you can deliver is likely to put you under stress.

Integration

Questions about your role in the world and how you might best position yourself to express your unique ideas may create pressure in you. While your
mind wants to concretize things, you may still feel some unresolved details
that you know you would feel more comfortable having resolved. Instead
of pushing yourself precipitously, wait. Smile inwardly as you recognize the
dance of the cosmic forces within that bring light and dark shadows into the
crevices of your awareness while you observe and wait to time your manifestation. Learn from past relationships and from emotional ups and downs.
Set intention without commitment while you visualize possibilities for the
future.

Evening Reflection: My Insights from Today

March 18, _____

Mental
Your questions frame how you think about reality.
Ask new questions in order to arrive at new answers.

Spiritual
Meditation time is essential to keep you balanced and aligned today.

Emotional
Feelings of others in your environment color your responses and your mood.
Things are not always what they seem.

Physical
Breathe shallowly and quietly. Imagine that the Divine breathes you.

Integration
When considering possible ways of being, what role is the role you want
to play going forward? Past experiences that shift your wisdom and understanding of your role in manifesting what you want to have happen for love,
happiness, and fulfillment are all important to recognize. The way you frame
those experiences make a difference in your consciousness moving forward.
When you connect with your understanding and remembrances, what kinds
of stories do you tell about those experiences? Is there another perspective,
another space you can move to in order to remember in another way?

Evening Reflection: My Insights from Today

_____

_____

_____

_____

_____

_____

_____

_____

March 19, _____

Mental
Information overload may challenge your inner knowing and direction.

Spiritual
Keep a beginner's mind when you interpret your feelings.
Remain open to all possibilities, including ones you never imagined before.

Emotional
Feelings change from moment to moment, depending on how you are
impacted by circumstances. Stay open but alert for reactions
that may lead you away from your true feelings.

Physical
You can easily overdo things today if you lose perspective of your own needs.

Integration
Make certain that your balance in the Mental, spiritual, emotional, and physical layers of being align. Stay alert to the way you integrate your past experiences into circumstances and relationships in your current life. Watch your breathing and your balance — use your physical sensitivity to assess your balance with sensitivity to the way decisions and actions lead you toward your long-term dreams. When aware of feelings or intuitions, where do they come from?

Evening Reflection: My Insights from Today

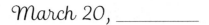
Mental

How you interpret information can change as you change your assumptions and
stories based on those assumptions. Be open to gathering new data
and try re-framing what you know in new ways.

Spiritual

At the depth of your inner Self, you know more than you think you know.
Take time alone to experience your depth and listen to your body's signals.

Emotional

Avoid emotional encounters that may provoke you in ways
that are incongruent with your aligned Self.
Be mindful, and recognize your vulnerabilities.

Physical

Listen to the signals from your body.
Pay attention to your pulse rate and how it varies with stress.

Integration

Put your attention on inner direction and alignment rather than action so
you gain dominion over your inner resources. What kind of inner resources
are your inner resources? Are you in a space that balances all components of
yourself? When you are open to the feelings of others on an intuitive level of
knowing, awareness operates on a deep collective level. When you sleep, you
are like one cell of the totality. As you recognize your connection with a collective consciousness, you may become increasingly aware of how those with
whom you interact affect you. Time alone is key to self-reflective awareness.
Take time for yourself.

Evening Reflection: My Insights from Today

_____

_____

_____

_____

_____

March 21, _____

Mental
Identify some areas of expertise you have and consider how to build on it.

Spiritual
How you treat yourself is how you treat others.

Emotional
Moods often transparently reflect your inner balance. Use the clues.

Physical
Your stamina and physical energy throughout the day reflects your health.

Integration
Because you live in multiple dimensions, you continually need to realign and readjust to internal and external circumstances and chemistry. Remaining dynamic and accepting of changes and instincts is healthy. Holding on to past ways of being may stifle your consciousness. How is your knowing different now from how it was a year ago at this time? five years ago? ten years ago? And what do you know now? From this point here now, what do you want to have happen?

Evening Reflection: My Insights from Today

March 22, _____

Mental
Build hypotheses from what you perceive
instead of drawing conclusions. Keep a beginner's mind.

Spiritual
Refine your perceptions to accommodate new possibilities.

Emotional
The Four Worlds balance you emotionally when they are aligned.
Put your inner relationship first.

Physical
Four Worlds balance you emotionally when they are aligned.
Put your inner relationship first.

Integration
What you know when you are out in the world may be different from what
you know when you're alone and internal. Pay attention to differences in your
knowing and opt to honor your inner Self. When in doubt, wait for clarity.

Evening Reflection: My Insights from Today

_____

_____

_____

_____

_____

_____

_____

_____

_____

_____

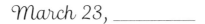

March 23, _____

Mental
Other people influence your thinking.
How do they affect your ideas?

Spiritual
Stay attuned to your body when you meditate.
Signals that whisper quietly speak loudly to your body.
Hear the "tells," and follow their lead.

Emotional
Subtle responses show how you are influenced
by people and circumstances.

Physical
Take a few quiet breaths to rebalance your body
before you react emotionally in situations that are stressful.

Integration
What you know deep inside on a gut level is ideally able to inform emotional reactions and impulses to take action. Use creative intelligence and your past experiences to perceive pressures that come from inside yourself vs. those that impact you from outside.

Evening Reflection: My Insights from Today

March 24, _____

Mental

Before you come to any conclusions about your thinking or feelings,
make sure you tune in to the still place deep inside yourself.

Spiritual

A sense of inner peacefulness can serve as a guide.
Feel it before you take any action.

Emotional

Let your intuition override your emotions today.
Speak only the deepest truths from your highest Self.

Physical

Use subtle signals from your body to indicate
where and how you are vulnerable.

Integration

Pressures on you toward actions may lead you astray unless you are aligned
internally with what feeds your soul and drives you toward your highest
goals. Stay alert and recognize your vulnerabilities.

Evening Reflection: My Insights from Today

_____

_____

_____

_____

_____

_____

_____

_____

_____

_____

March 25, _____

Mental

Notice how your ideas shift when you are with other people.

Spiritual

You know when energy around you is aligned
and congruent with your deepest Self and when it is not.
Take time to recognize what you know.
And ask, "What do I know now?"

Emotional

Stay aware of your reactions to others
and avoid being provoked by or provoking others.

Physical

Avoid all physical overindulgences.

Integration

Your internal sense of comfort and energetic balance is important. Stay true to yourself and to the values you stand for. Reactivity may be high around you. Stay alert and stay internal.

Evening Reflection: My Insights from Today

_____

_____

_____

_____

_____

_____

_____

_____

March 26, _____

Mental

Premature opinions influence what you perceive and grasp in the moment.
Mull things over.

Spiritual

Connecting with your deepest core Self aligns you toward health.

Emotional

Stay emotionally balanced despite outside pressures.

Physical

Smells provide cellular indicators for your body's immune health
and wellbeing. Essential oils may be of value to balance your energy.

Integration

Review the *Axes of Awareness* (see resources on page 373), so you understand
the importance of recognizing the way your emotional instincts interface
with your body instincts. How you orient your thinking is crucial to your
consciousness and to manifesting your true intentions.

Evening Reflection: My Insights from Today

_____

_____

_____

_____

_____

_____

_____

_____

_____

_____

_____

March 27, _____

Mental
Keep in mind that circumstances and their challenges
provide opportunities for growth of Self-awareness.

Spiritual
Putting your inner Self first to find true balance relieves others
from the responsibility of caring for you.

Emotional
Emotional reactivity may challenge your emotional balance.
Use your words carefully.

Physical
Continued monitoring of physical health requires alertness of all your senses.

Integration
With the pressures of the day impacting your vulnerabilities, it is essential
that you take time to recognize and reflect on what you already know about
yourself and use your inner voice of wisdom as a guide to your actions.

Evening Reflection: My Insights from Today

March 28, _____

Mental
Challenges that push you to rethink your ways of perceiving the world also push you to achieve more of yourself.

Spiritual
Your inner voice whispers gently like a breeze. You can easily miss hearing it. Take time to listen by setting aside time for meditation.

Emotional
Your balance between your body/instinct/mind and feeling/instinct/mind is important to understand. Take time to reflect on it.

Physical
Physical overload presents some dangers today.

Integration
Words, once spoken, take form both inside you and in other people. Be careful in how you communicate, and always ask if your communication aligns with what you want to have happen and how it might impact you and the other person receiving it. Be mindfully alert.

Evening Reflection: My Insights from Today

_____

_____

_____

_____

_____

_____

_____

_____

_____

_____

March 29, _____

Mental
Avoid action until you are certain that all layers of yourself balance.

Spiritual
Be receptive to learning new things about yourself. Take in new information, and hold it inside while you allow it to steep and ripen.

Emotional
A single standard for yourself and others reflects inner congruence.

Physical
Exercise and eat with great discipline. Avoid social eating.

Integration
When you experience balance in yourself, that's like what? When balanced, how do you know you are balanced? Keep these questions in mind throughout the day, and check in with your responses periodically.

Evening Reflection: My Insights from Today

March 30, _____

Mental
Avoid committing to action until you are certain
that all layers of yourself balance.

Spiritual
Use inner wisdom to guide insights about yourself.

Emotional
Take action if you know that your intuition is reliable
and listen to it when it speaks.

Physical
Pay attention to the tension in your body and use it to adjust your energy.

Integration
Pressures and stress may push you toward action. Be alert to your inner process and take actions when they align congruently with your intentions, otherwise stay with what you know works for you and wait until you feel certain and clear about your actions.

Evening Reflection: My Insights from Today

_____

_____

_____

_____

_____

_____

_____

_____

_____

_____

_____

March 31, _____

Mental

Balance the body/instinct/mind and feeling/instinct/mind carefully.
You are vulnerable to misinterpretations.

Spiritual

Meditate, breathe deeply, and get enough rest and sleep.

Emotional

Openness to the feelings of others makes you vulnerable to their moods.

Physical

You are sensitive and vulnerable to outside influences.
Be protective of your body and what you know supports your health.

Integration

Self-reflection and self-knowledge can protect you from stress and misperceptions. Use your inner voice to align you based on your past experiences and self-knowledge. Be compassionate and kind to yourself and avoid stressful situations and people.

Evening Reflection: My Insights from Today

April 1, _____

Mental
Use this time to put together your thoughts and to recognize how you can release limiting beliefs for better alignment. Be cautious with words.

Spiritual
What do you know about your inner balance now?

Emotional
When emotional, what happened just before you experienced emotions?

Physical
Take time to attend to your body without judgment, acknowledging your sensitivities.

Integration
Use your higher mind to assess what honors your highest goals. You may be in conflict. If in doubt, wait.

Evening Reflection: My Insights from Today

_____

_____

_____

_____

_____

_____

_____

_____

_____

_____

_____

_____

April 2, _____

Mental
What do you know about tension between
your body, mind, spirit, and emotions now?

Spiritual
Focus during meditation on your inner balance
and how you know when body, mind and spirit are balanced.
Ask, "When in alignment at all levels of my Self, that's like what?"

Emotional
When around others, you may be vulnerable and super sensitive.
Recognize what you feel, but err on the side of silence and inaction.

Physical
Stay quiet and rest more than you think you should.

Integration
Action that comes from a deep knowing within the core of your being may
be aligned. Check your emotions to be certain, before taking action, that you
have visualized what you want to have happen and that it aligns on all layers
of your being.

Evening Reflection: My Insights from Today

April 3, _____

Mental
Reframe your thoughts in new positively loving ways.
Be creative. Use words sparingly.

Spiritual
Take care of yourself with meditation. Focus on the balance between your body
and your spirit. What do you know from that space of balance?

Emotional
Avoid overindulging in any way, i.e., be still and self-disciplined.
You are sensitive to the feelings of others.

Physical
Time to rest and regenerate your energy is essential to health.
Take that time.

Integration
The way you balance body/instinct/mind and feelings/instinct/mind is critical
to your clarity. Take a bit more time to consider your possible actions before
you commit to any path.

Evening Reflection: My Insights from Today

_____

_____

_____

_____

_____

_____

_____

_____

_____

_____

_____

April 4, _____

Mental
You know more than you think you know.
Open new pathways in your thinking.

Spiritual
During meditation, limit your attention by stilling your breath
until you feel that the Divine breathes you.

Emotional
Consider the importance of your nonverbal "tells,"
and pay attention to them within yourself.

Physical
You are sensitive physically. Use your body "tells" and listen to your body.

Integration
You are likely to feel most empowered when you center yourself internally
prior to going about your day. Time to recognize your deep Self is time that
empowers you at your core.

Evening Reflection: My Insights from Today

April 5, _____

Mental
Opening to possibilities by thinking in new ways
allows your intuition to penetrate your mind.

Spiritual
Tap into your gut to align your sense of Self,
which puts you in energetic attunement.

Emotional
Stay alert to your needs despite high sensitivity to the feelings of others.

Physical
Promising more than you can deliver endangers your health
and creates stress.

Integration
Listen carefully for the inner voice that whispers gently to you during your
day. Still your body and penetrate to the depth of inner knowing when stress
impacts you. Be meditative before any action.

Evening Reflection: My Insights from Today

April 6, _____

Mental

When challenges repeat in your life, you gain a new opportunity to reframe your thinking and make choices that are new, positive, and creative.

Spiritual

Stay focused on the moment and limit your attention toward aligning your inner Self to balance and health.

Emotional

Transforming emotions may require "walking in the other person's shoes." Do so mindfully.

Physical

Note a few things that energize you and a few things that deplete you. What do you notice about what you have noted?

Integration

Balancing all parts of yourself can be tricky unless you center and honor your deep Self. Remember that how you care for yourself is how you care for others. Be kind by modeling good self-care and self-responsibility.

Evening Reflection: My Insights from Today

_____

_____

_____

_____

_____

_____

_____

_____

_____

_____

April 7, _____

Mental

Too much information may be confusing
and may limit your creative possibilities.

Spiritual

What beliefs about yourself limit you?

Emotional

What do you know about how other people impact your emotions?

Physical

When you feel stress, what kind of stress is in your body?

Integration

Listening to the signals you receive from your body and putting your attention on them can help you orient your thoughts in ways that facilitate balance at a deep level of yourself. Use your own process as your guide by taking time alone to meditate and focus on what your body tells you. Claim your inner authority.

Evening Reflection: My Insights from Today

April 8, _____

Mental
Limitations on your thoughts may put pressure on you that is unnecessary.
Keep a bird's eye view.

Spiritual
Value your sensitivities and respect them.

Emotional
Feelings change with awareness.
You have the power internally to change negative feelings to positive ones.

Physical
Your body requirements may be different from your desires.
Pay attention to the choices you make.

Integration
Because of your shifting sensitivities, it is important that you recognize how important timing is, and pay attention to the openness of others to you. What you want to have happen may be different from what others want to have happen. What do you want to manifest and how do your responses support that?

Evening Reflection: My Insights from Today

April 9, _____

Mental
Formulate ideas for later use, but be careful to remain silent about them.

Spiritual
Your inner voice of wisdom encourages compassion toward Self and others.

Emotional
Emotional awareness transforms past reflection
into positive future projections.

Physical
What do you know about what your body needs now?
Ask this question throughout your day.

Integration
Before you know what is correct for you to manifest, it is essential to ask questions of your inner deep Self. A key question today is, "What revisions in my thinking might empower me toward achieving my highest goals?" Focus on this question during meditation.

Evening Reflection: My Insights from Today

_____

_____

_____

_____

_____

_____

_____

_____

_____

_____

_____

April 10, _____

Mental
How you do anything, is how you do everything.
Take dominion over your life. Use your resources mindfully.

Spiritual
Take charge of your inner Self by remaining still until you recognize
and balance your emotions. Words, once spoken, create form.
Refrain from speaking lightly.

Emotional
It is only when you limit your reactions and expand your consciousness
that deep awareness brings you into a new future.

Physical
Pay special attention to your eating, especially when in social situations.

Integration
Balance and integrated alignment as a multidimensional being depends on
patience and mindful attention to how the parts of yourself communicate
with each other. Before you take any action or react impulsively, take a few
breaths while you recognize and acknowledge your deep Self and higher
purpose. Align at that level of your consciousness.

Evening Reflection: My Insights from Today

April 11, _____

Mental

Your mind creates stories to help you make sense of
what happens around you. Change your story and you change your world.
Play with new stories and new "spins" on your life story.
Be mindful as you experience what changes.

Spiritual

Speak to yourself with your inner voice that guides you
toward wisdom and understanding with love.

Emotional

Emotional balance that honors your inner integrity
and purpose shifts reactivity.

Physical

Balancing body/feelings/instinct/mind reduces stress
and enhances health, communicating about body reserves and resources.

Integration

Balancing yourself requires acute discernment of what you want to have happen and what is likely to happen in reality. Read the "tells" for yourself in others before you commit to any path of action.

Evening Reflection: My Insights from Today

April 12, _____

Mental
Details often help clarify things in your decision process.
Get details you need.

Spiritual
Emotional reactions that trigger your inner voice of wisdom give you important
information on which you can focus for clarity.

Emotional
Review repeating patterns in life experiences
to access cycles important to you.

Physical
Physical timing relates to your chemistry.
Pay attention to your body balance.

Integration
So much of what manifests in your life depends on the way you frame your
thoughts and reactions. Err on the side of inaction rather than on the side of
impulsive reactivity. Listen to your inner voice and be as kind to yourself as
you wish others were kind to you.

Evening Reflection: My Insights from Today

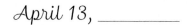

April 13, _____

Mental
Focus and detail helps clarify decisions. Pay attention and ask for the details you need so you can plan ahead for yourself properly.

Spiritual
Self-care is essential to the care of others.
Focus on your inner smile that enhances your sense of worth.

Emotional
Use healthy emotions to buoy you up when you begin to question your feelings. Avoid impulsive reactivity.

Physical
Enhance physical health by practicing visualizations of healthy life practices.

Integration
Because you may be open and vulnerable to the energy and feelings of others, it is important to ground yourself in what you already know about yourself and your reality. Remain vigilant to new information so you can change your orientation and actions accordingly.

Evening Reflection: My Insights from Today

April 14, _____

Mental

Consider what limitations on you are realistic.
Expand where you can, and accept what is realistic.

Spiritual

Use your intuitive Self to sense what path might best be for you.

Emotional

Strength of Self comes from your inner core of knowing. Use it.

Physical

Pushing yourself beyond your comfort zone can backfire strongly today.

Integration

Understanding the balance between body/instinct/mind and feeling/instinct/mind is extremely helpful in giving you a way to understand your reactions and make choices about them. Read the *Axes of Awareness* (see resources on page 373) to gain insight into how this dynamic works in you. It is worth the effort, especially today.

Evening Reflection: My Insights from Today

April 15, _____

Mental

Recognize the necessity of limitations in order keep perspective in life.

Spiritual

Surrendering to your higher Self sometimes requires discipline
and self-management. Take time alone to tune in to your divine core.

Emotional

Empathy for the needs expressed by others
must balance with your own needs.

Physical

You know your limitations physically. Keep them in mind
and avoid pushing your body when it gives you subtle "tells."

Integration

Self-discipline allows your intuition to guide your words and actions in
ways that honor your highest goals. Limitation focuses attention on what is
important so you can move forward from that place in yourself of clarity and
superconscious knowledge. Use your inner wisdom.

Evening Reflection: My Insights from Today

_____

_____

_____

_____

_____

_____

_____

_____

_____

_____

April 16, _____

Mental

What you think and what you feel may be a bit out of sync.
Take time to tune in to what you want to have happen
and consider the impact of what you think and say.

Spiritual

Stay internal and very quiet today.
Tap into your inner wisdom that attunes you to your deepest values.

Emotional

Emotions run high. Withdraw into yourself to maintain inner resources.

Physical

Balancing your energy so you expend only
what you can afford to spend enhances your health.

Integration

Consider the question, "What do you know about your relationship limitations and healing?" Ask this question of yourself six times so you move through different layers of awareness within yourself when you ask it. Write your answers down. Then, ask if there is an action you would like to take from that space there.

Evening Reflection: My Insights from Today

_____

_____

_____

_____

_____

_____

_____

_____

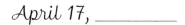

Mental

Use your intuition and instinct to inform your thoughts, and use your creative intelligence to envision a future that honors your highest goals.

Spiritual

Recognize and apply loving kindness in inner communication,
and use it to build your inner strength.

Emotional

Emotions run high. Monitor communication that assures self-discipline.

Physical

Physical limitations may be frustrating but they may protect your health.

Integration

Take time to consider what emotionally triggers you before you speak. It is essential to your consciousness that you apply mindful creative intelligence to your emotions so they express your highest goals and principles rather than the momentary frustrations of daily life. Be wise in how you manage yourself. You are a role model to others. Be your best Self.

Evening Reflection: My Insights from Today

April 18, _____

Mental
Reframe self-talk to change your self-image. Open to new possibilities.

Spiritual
You align to multidimensional Worlds.
Recognize that they turn on and off in you all the time.

Emotional
When you are aware of others,
you are empathic without reacting impulsively from it.

Physical
Limit physical exertion today; watch your heart rate while exercising.

Integration
Influences and pressures of the day may move you away from yourself in ways that surprise you if you lose focus of what is important. Take time for yourself to center and realign to your inner values. Keep your focus on what you want to have happen. Be the person you aspire to be and let your spirit guide you.

Evening Reflection: My Insights from Today

April 19, _____

Mental
Use this time to take stock of your strengths and anchor them in your mind.

Spiritual
How you care for yourself is how you care for others.
Take time to meditate and focus on yourself. It pays dividends.

Emotional
You know more about your true Self than anyone else.
"What do you know about your spiritual Self now?"

Physical
Energetic depletion is a risk when you do more
than you know is healthy for you.

Integration
You may find yourself in situations that put you in conflict and put you under stress. To reduce stress, look for new ways to frame your stories so you balance and express emotions in ways that reflect love rather than judgment. Make no assumptions. Speak kindly at all times.

Evening Reflection: My Insights from Today

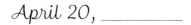

April 20, _____

Mental

When you function at your strongest and best, that's like what?

Spiritual

When guided by spirit in your life, what do you know about how you know what you know? Meditate and focus on this question.

Emotional

You are open to the energies and input of others.
Be aware of what you feel and how you feel when you are alone compared to when in the presence of other people or animals.

Physical

Be especially careful regarding your eating today.

Integration

You know more and have more inner resilience than you think or feel. Take a stand for yourself and listen to your feelings. Express them mindfully and with loving energy rather than with reactively. Be as sensitive to the feelings of others as you want them to be of yours. Use words with care.

Evening Reflection: My Insights from Today

April 21, _____

Mental
Pose new questions that can lead to expansive ways of understanding.

Spiritual
Stay focused on your needs and desires before tuning in to others.

Emotional
Breathing is key to monitoring emotional stress and releasing it.

Physical
Use your energy wisely. Take time to meditate and rest.

Integration
Your deep sensitivity to others may activate emotions that pull you away from yourself. Consider your requirements, needs, and wants. When you care for yourself with respect and sensitivity, you care for others as well.

Evening Reflection: My Insights from Today

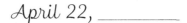

April 22, _____

Mental
Use this time as an opportunity to envision a positive future
for yourself despite stress around you.

Spiritual
Remain focused on inner wisdom for guidance.

Emotional
When you live aligned with your values, you feel at ease.

Physical
Anxiety often alerts you to misalignment of your energy
or of situational pressures.

Integration
Remaining true to your inner values and principles despite outside stress
allows you to envision new outcomes in daily situations that may align in new
ways. All challenges are opportunities for change and growth. Use them well
and with inner wisdom.

Evening Reflection: My Insights from Today

April 23, _____

Mental
Use your creative mind to monitor
and reorient to unexpected twists and turns during the day.

Spiritual
When you struggle against what you know balances you,
you are likely to feel tension inside and disharmony with others.

Emotional
Monitor your feelings to assure they honor your core values.

Physical
Put positive focus on physical health to build energy reserves.

Integration
Take the time you need to gain inner clarity so you balance your values and
self-care with challenges facing you in your life. When in doubt about what
is "right" for you, take a few moments to breathe and ask yourself "what do
I know now?" Operate from within and from the wisdom deep within your
heart and soul.

Evening Reflection: My Insights from Today

April 24, _____

Mental

Pressures from others may overwhelm inner resolve to find your own path.

Spiritual

The use of breathing in meditation is likely to be beneficial
in accessing your inner wisdom today. Let the Divine breathe you.

Emotional

Self-esteem grows when your feelings count as much as the feelings of others.

Physical

Avoid social eating and drinking that may tend toward overindulgence.

Integration

Be mindful of taking time to care for yourself. Tools that helped you in the past are likely to help you again. The *Axes of Awareness* (see resources on page 373) is an important concept to understand and to utilize on a day like today when you are vulnerable to the energy around you and have to discern what feelings "belong" to you and what you are picking up on from those around you. Be cautious and use words sparingly.

Evening Reflection: My Insights from Today

Mental
Piece some new ideas together
without needing to understand the whole picture.

Spiritual
Remaining receptive to new perspectives and to the inner stirrings
of your heart open you to realignment.

Emotional
Social situations that validate your experiences and connect you
to your deepest sense of Self are ones you can trust.

Physical
Be wary of overextending yourself. Conserve your energy.

Integration
Because you are a multidimensional being, it is important to recognize how
you balance your Mental, Spiritual, Emotional, and Physical Worlds or layers
of consciousness. Taking time to meditate daily and to tune in to your deep
Self allows the worlds to unify and balance effortlessly. A few moments to
re-center during your day helps this process.

Evening Reflection: My Insights from Today

April 26, _____

Mental
Expect the unexpected and align your inner mind
for whatever comes your way.

Spiritual
Commitment to your inner process is key in balancing consciously.

Emotional
Consciousness relies on recognition of consequences
when you put yourself last.

Physical
Listening to the cycle of your body allows you to balance rest and activity.

Integration
Sensitivity to the needs of others may pull you away from your own needs.
It is the balance and alignment of mutual needs and fulfillment of them that
allows relationships to thrive and deepen. Be mindful of your communications and of how you describe your requirements, needs, and wants to those
about whom you care. Respect differences and honor connected alignment.

Evening Reflection: My Insights from Today

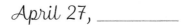

April 27, _____

Mental
Pay attention to how other people influence your thinking,
and act appropriately.

Spiritual
Recognize that core responses guide your sense of
what aligns with you and what you express in the world.

Emotional
Values are key to conscious interactions and intentional planning.

Physical
Balance of the body/instinct/mind and feelings/instinct/mind
is crucial to consider in planning your day.

Integration
What do you know now about your inner and outer alignment? When you are
aligned and honoring your core values, that's like what? Take time to answer
these questions and write your answers down. What do you notice about the
words you use? Is there anything else you know now?

Evening Reflection: My Insights from Today

_____

_____

_____

_____

_____

_____

_____

_____

_____

_____

_____

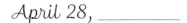

April 28, _____

Mental

The four ways of being refer to the Four Worlds. Remember that you live
in all dimensions of reality and must balance in all to feel fulfilled.

Spiritual

Listen to your "story" from the depth of yourself
and use the lessons of your life for growth.

Emotional

Pay attention to what happens to you when you are with others who express
strong emotions. Stay within your own comfort zone and avoid reactivity.

Physical

Eat with discipline and care, especially when in social situations.
Rest more than you think you should.

Integration

Consciousness relies on discernment of yourself and of your perceptions in
situations that challenge you mentally, spiritually, emotionally, and physically. Rely on your past experiences to inform the present and be more cautious than usual before acting.

Evening Reflection: My Insights from Today

_____

_____

_____

_____

_____

_____

_____

_____

_____

April 29, _____

Mental
Questions are more crucial than answers.
Pose questions about your perceptions in new ways.

Spiritual
Find a positive internal place and meditate from there.

Emotional
Essential oils can help balance your energies.
Put yourself only into situations that you know are healthy for you,
and avoid emotionally stressful circumstances.

Physical
Anchor positive physical gains by noting them and reinforcing them.

Integration
Use your soft intuitive whisper to warn you of situations that are unhealthy
for you. Pay attention. Meditate extra and with attention on your physical
balance, as it enhances and can build reserves in aligning your energy. Be
mindful throughout your day.

Evening Reflection: My Insights from Today

April 30, _____

Mental
What you think now becomes reality at the end of July.
Remain open to new viewpoints and be willing to change your own.

Spiritual
Use your senses to tap into awareness of what resonates with you.

Emotional
Watch your emotional responses for signs of stress.
Be on alert for emotional reactivity.

Physical
You are physically vulnerable today. Take time to attend to your body.

Integration
Lots of information and questions may stream into your mind, causing confusion and activating new possibilities for the future. Let your mind take in all perspectives and take time alone to let go of it all as your deeper creative intelligence processes it all. Have some fun. Play. Laugh. Be in the cosmic joke with it and enjoy the ride.

Evening Reflection: My Insights from Today

May 1, _____

Mental

Consider how your thinking contributes to your Mental, Spiritual, Emotional, and Physical health. Rethink areas that are out of balance.

Spiritual

Your body communicates subtly to your inner Self. Take the time to be still and meditate. Stay focused on your inner truth and follow its lead.

Emotional

Emotions of others affect you. Note how the way others speak to you activates inner communication in you. Be mindful.

Physical

Your senses are especially acute today.
Pay attention to what your body tells you.

Integration

Put attention to integrating past experiences as they relate to your present and future plans. Consider how your plans and feelings affect others. Continue thinking creatively, adding a new spin to old ideas. You remain deeply open when you sleep to the influences of the collective archetypes, yet, you also have the capacity in your waking life to interpret your feelings using your discriminative capacity. Use practical discernment in your world of instincts and how they might play out. Continue to be aware. Use the day to rest from any activities of the past week.

Evening Reflection: My Insights from Today

May 2, _____

Mental
Use your intelligence to call upon what worked well for you in the past.

Spiritual
Caring for yourself before taking care of others models self-responsibility. Listen for your inner voice of wisdom.

Emotional
Caring for yourself before taking care of others models self-responsibility. Listen for your inner voice of wisdom.

Physical
Balance physically by listening to yourself rather than reacting to outside pressures.

Integration
When you limit your activities and your focus to what is important, you gain perspective on how you can move forward effectively. Too much information may put you on overload. Take time to align and balance before you start your day, and rebalance regularly throughout your day so you stay centered and in your core strength.

Evening Reflection: My Insights from Today

May 3, _____

Mental
New innovative questions can lead to unexpected answers.

Spiritual
Remaining open to new ways of perceiving widens your perspectives and may lead you to new awareness about yourself.

Emotional
Emotional volatility around you impacts your perceptions.

Physical
Rest and relaxation are important to your health.

Integration
Spiritual wisdom that informs correct action develops over time. Begin thinking about what inspires you toward achieving your deepest goals. Follow your heart more than your mind, and limit your options while discerning what you truly value. You are more able to determine what is right for you than anyone else. Follow your inner voice of wisdom, being gentle and kind with yourself. Help others who need clarity in gentle ways as well.

Evening Reflection: My Insights from Today

May 4, _____

Mental
Consider the long-term ramifications of impulsive actions.

Spiritual
Recognize that words affect your inner perceptions
so monitor self-talk carefully.

Emotional
Pressure from others may create stress on you that results
in you doubting your own perceptions and feelings.

Physical
Limitations on you physically as well as emotionally create anxiety in you.

Integration
Doubts about yourself and your direction may surface undermining your confidence and self-assurance. Be open to your doubts and consider them in terms of your past experiences and whether they can inform your present. Be careful in how you talk to yourself and other people. Words carry energy that affect self-perceptions. Use your words with love and kindness. Recognize that you are in the process of self-discovery as are others around you.

Evening Reflection: My Insights from Today

May 5, _____

Mental
Information overload may result in precipitous action.
Take your time to think things through.

Spiritual
Listen to how your needs reflect the needs of others.
Be aware of your own needs first.

Emotional
Feelings must facilitate ease and relaxation in order to be healthy.

Physical
Pushing yourself when you need rest and time alone may drain your energy.
Take time you need to refresh and realign.

Integration
Consider how you might best use your inner resources and skills to move forward in what you want to have happen. Ask yourself, "When I'm following my inner direction of Self, that's like what? When I'm creatively inspired, that's like what?" Listen to your answers and let them inform the planning for your next steps toward reaching your highest goal.

Evening Reflection: My Insights from Today

May 6, _____

Mental
Not everything is as it seems. Stay in touch with your inner direction
and look for ways you can manifest it.

Spiritual
Maintain an attitude of inner creativity while exploring new possibilities.

Emotional
Avoid emotional confrontations that may undermine your inner Self.

Physical
Stay with what you know works for your body
and err on the side of rest rather than activity.

Integration
Taking time to tune in to your inner Self is essential in determining any
course of action prior to committing to it. Your breathing is a key to how balanced and at ease you are as you move through your day. Listen for your still
Self, and, when in doubt, pay attention to how your breathing is. Still your
breath and use the "hook-up" to realign. Listen to your inner voice moving
from that place to maximize your resources and to act from clarity.

Evening Reflection: My Insights from Today

May 7, _____

Mental
Avoid taking action in response to outside pressures.

Spiritual
Use past experiences as your guide in tuning in to your intuition.
Rely on what you already know works for you.

Emotional
Align in your life so supportive people help you build a base of confidence.

Physical
Rely on past body signals for information today. Eat with discipline.

Integration
You know more than you think you know, so tap into the inner depths of
yourself as a guide for orienting yourself. Be wary about speaking prematurely about your feelings, especially when emotionally triggered by circumstances and people around you. Err on the side of less rather than more
activity today.

Evening Reflection: My Insights from Today

_____

_____

_____

_____

_____

_____

_____

_____

_____

_____

_____

May 8, _____

Mental
Observe and form hypotheses, but be patient with yourself.
Draw no conclusions.

Spiritual
Try on new possibilities and imagine all of them without taking action.

Emotional
Recognize emotions without committing to any direction for their expression.

Physical
Pay attention to your body and breathing,
your sense of smell, your stamina, and your diet.

Integration
Your emotions may tell you one thing and your intuition may tell you something else. Be mindful of saying or doing too much if you have any emotional reactions that raise red flags about your inner balance and clarity. Wait for clear inner signals.

Evening Reflection: My Insights from Today

May 9, _____

Mental
Watch for "tells" about your reactions to various situations.

Spiritual
Time alone to tune in to your inner process, values,
and direction is key to balance.

Emotional
Emotions of others may push your buttons. Be on alert and be mindful
of what you want to have happen in each interaction.

Physical
Protect your immune system by avoiding any physical stressors.

Integration
The following quote from Steve Jobs' 2005 Stanford Commencement address
is applicable for orienting you today. He said, "You can't connect the dots
looking forward; you can only connect them looking backwards. So you have
to trust that the dots will somehow connect in your future." Listen to your
inner stories and ask, "What do I know now?"

Evening Reflection: My Insights from Today

_____

_____

_____

_____

_____

_____

_____

_____

_____

_____

May 10, _____

Mental
Protect your immune system by avoiding any physical stressors.

Spiritual
New perspectives are easier to take in when you seek inner clarity
and open yourself up to new ways of being.

Emotional
Reactions of other people are likely to be more about them than about you.
Avoid taking the responses of others personally,
but remain mindful of your role in relationships.

Physical
Feeling depleted is likely if you take on more than the day supports.

Integration
You may find yourself questioning your core values and assumptions as you seek balance and inner clarity. Allow your thoughts to expand and, at the same time, let them go so new thoughts and perceptions can replace outworn ideas.

Evening Reflection: My Insights from Today

May 11, _____

Mental
Consider what is most important to you when you contemplate
any action or express your thoughts in words.

Spiritual
Lack of internal clarity about yourself allows you to be open
to other perspectives.

Emotional
Deepening emotional awareness is part of a wider evolutionary process.

Physical
Feeling depleted is likely if you take on more than the day supports.

Integration
Allow your spiritual principles and higher Self to guide any actions you might
consider taking. Visualize what you want to happen and how you want to
position yourself before you make any commitments.

Evening Reflection: My Insights from Today

May 12, _____

Mental
Mental pressures drive you.
Register ideas but wait to act while they germinate.

Spiritual
Stay focused on your inner path, despite outside pressures.

Emotional
Balanced emotions require recognizing
polarized viewpoints as equally valid.

Physical
Balanced emotions require recognizing
polarized viewpoints as equally valid.

Integration
Use this time to tune in to your inner guides during meditation and reorient
yourself in new ways. Use your mind to re-vision your past in recognizing
that you always have choice in how you remember and what you learn from
your experiences. Be creative and positive.

Evening Reflection: My Insights from Today

May 13, _____

Mental

Your mind influences others as well as yourself.
Remain unattached to how others perceive you.

Spiritual

The vision you have for yourself is essential to your success.
Stay true to yourself.

Emotional

Clarify whether your mind/body balance is congruent with your deepest goals.

Physical

Acting instinctively and mindlessly may prove physically depleting.

Integration

Conflicts between your needs and those about whom you care deeply may
challenge your resolve to honor yourself. Be strong within by taking quiet
contemplative time alone. Recognize what you know about your needs and
honor them. Those who respect you respect your needs and wisdom.

Evening Reflection: My Insights from Today

May 14, _____

Mental

Consider what you tell yourself. The way you use internal language impacts how you perceive yourself and others.

Spiritual

Subconscious thoughts become reality. Remain positive and optimistic.

Emotional

Be mindful of the balance between your body awareness
and your emotions. Monitor this balance for alignment.

Physical

Pushing yourself is risky. Take time to refresh your energy.

Integration

Tap in to what you already know about yourself. Ask, "What do I know about
my inner story? Is there a space inside me that is peaceful and balanced?
What do I know about that space now?" Take time alone to self-reflect.

Evening Reflection: My Insights from Today

_____

_____

_____

_____

_____

_____

_____

_____

_____

_____

May 15, _____

Mental
Because you are open and sensitive to the energy around you,
it is essential that you stay aware of your unique perspective.

Spiritual
How you care for yourself is how you care for others.
Be as protective of yourself as you are of those you love.

Emotional
Avoid taking on the emotions of others unless they also serve your needs.

Physical
Emotional stress may affect your eating and exercise.
Pay attention to your body.

Integration
How you connect with and care for others is an expression of your values.
Take care of yourself as you take care of others and be mindful of your inner
balance as you move through your activities.

Evening Reflection: My Insights from Today

_____

_____

_____

_____

_____

_____

_____

_____

_____

_____

May 16, _____

Mental
Visualize what you want to manifest while imagining how this vision will make you feel. Ask: "And when _____, then what happens?"

Spiritual
By taking time for yourself in meditation,
you strengthen the depth of yourself-awareness.

Emotional
Trust yourself and avoid being pulled by the emotions of others.

Physical
Be kind to your body by getting extra rest and being sensitive
to its needs rather than to the activities around you.

Integration
It is always wise to tune into the depth of yourself to determine what you want to have happen and how you want it to happen. Listen for your inner voice that knows with clarity. Remember that when in doubt you are unclear and need time to gain clarity and self-direction. Take that time in whatever way best serves you.

Evening Reflection: My Insights from Today

May 17, _____

Mental

Recalling past times that felt as confusing as today may be reassuring.

Spiritual

You are highly empathic today and pick up on what others feel.
Take extra time alone.

Emotional

You may feel emotionally driven by feelings and ideas of others.
Consider your reactivity before you speak or act.

Physical

Acting instinctively and mindlessly may prove physically depleting.

Integration

Stay connected to your highest goals and when you are unclear about your next step forward, take time to ask, "What do I know about what I want to have happen now?" This question alone is potent in turning your attention back to your inner core of Self so you refocus and realign at a deep level of yourself. Use this question often.

Evening Reflection: My Insights from Today

May 18, _____

Mental
What role do you want to play in influencing others?

Spiritual
Tune in to yourself when you are alone to avoid undue influence of others.

Emotional
Trust emotions only if you feel harmonious and at ease.

Physical
Quiet time is important to your physical health.
Make sure you take time to rebalance several times during the day.

Integration
Some self-doubt about what you really want to do or not do on the instinctive level is natural as you wonder about your choices and direction. Considering all possibilities is part of the process that brings clarity about the best path for you. Look to your body for answers since it tells you what and how you feel. Take time alone, i.e., away from others, to be clear about your feelings and your health. Rely on past self-awareness. Use this information as instructive. Be wary of overexercising.

Evening Reflection: My Insights from Today

May 19, _____

Mental
Consider many alternative viewpoints before coming to any conclusions.

Spiritual
Deep self-awareness often emerges after you take time for inner reflection.

Emotional
Other people influence in subtle and not so subtle ways.
Stay mindful of your own needs.

Physical
Pushing your body may drive you beyond what is healthy for you.

Integration
Emotional connections may drive you both positively and negatively. Be mindful and alert to how emotions impact your feelings about yourself and your thinking. Words carry energy, so use them carefully with attention to their impact. Frame your language positively and let your words carry kindness and compassion.

Evening Reflection: My Insights from Today

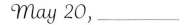
Mental
Patience serves you well while you ask questions
and seek clarity of thought.

Spiritual
Inner alignment in service of your life vision always serves you well.

Emotional
Twists and turns of the day require
emotional awareness to achieve balance.

Physical
Breathe through the day as a way to integrate
your mind and find balance.

Integration
Trying to please others can derail you from what is most important for you.
Stay clear within yourself by listening to your inner voice of wisdom and
by taking time to consider the language you use internally. What is most
important to you now? When aligned and balanced, that's like what?

Evening Reflection: My Insights from Today

_____

_____

_____

_____

_____

_____

_____

_____

_____

_____

May 21, _____

Mental
Actions based in grounded choices and awareness are well planned.

Spiritual
Meditation is important in anchoring your self-awareness.
Make it a priority.

Emotional
Take authority over your emotions so you remain balanced
even when feeling pressure to act.

Physical
Take a few extra moments to breathe through stress to find balance.

Integration
In order to make clear choices, it is essential that you discern information, accurately freeing yourself from errors that color your perceptions with unfounded desires. Examine your choices carefully. Take time to self-reflect and ask questions to be certain that you are properly oriented toward your goals. Are you in the right frame of mind? Are you moving in the right direction? What do you want to have happen? Consider these questions and reorient appropriately.

Evening Reflection: My Insights from Today

_____

_____

_____

_____

_____

_____

_____

_____

May 22, _____

Mental
Consider how your actions might play out prior to implementing them.

Spiritual
Identify what you want to have happen and what those you care about might want to have happen before you take any action.

Emotional
Watch for inner pressure that push you to verbalize prematurely.

Physical
Stress is your signal that you have overextended yourself. Take it seriously.

Integration
Inner authority and strength comes from knowing that your actions are rooted in clarity of purpose and self-knowledge. Rely on what you know works for you and listen to the inner voice of Knowing to guide your direction and movement toward your highest goals. Be wise about how you spend your energy.

Evening Reflection: My Insights from Today

Mental

Recognize that you tap into your deepest Self when you
call upon a wider scope of knowledge than you grasp.

Spiritual

When you sleep, you are connected to all living consciousness.
Allow expansion.

Emotional

You are sensitive to the needs and feelings of others around you.
Be empathic but remain true to your own guiding principles and values.
Maintain your inner harmony and balance.

Physical

Respect your physical boundaries and limitations
with discipline and gratitude.

Integration

When you are most alert to your inner instincts and wisdom, that's like
what? What do you know about your deepest Self? Take time to answer these
questions today. It is most crucial that you use your inner knowing to guide
you toward balance and clarity. You are unique and special. Call forth that
brilliance.

Evening Reflection: My Insights from Today

_____

_____

_____

_____

_____

_____

_____

_____

_____

_____

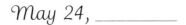

May 24, _____

Mental
You know more than you think you know.
Open your mind to new possibilities. Think outside the box.

Spiritual
Stay with what you know about your inner direction and goals,
and avoid being influenced by circumstances and people around you.

Emotional
What others tell you is best heard when you listen
with your inner Self rather than from your emotions.

Physical
An inner smile can balance your body
through its positive message and energy.

Integration
Balancing your body/instinct/mind and feeling/instinct/mind *Axes of Awareness* (see resources on page 373) is crucial today. Take time to reorient and breathe. Limit your activities to so you have time to assure that your intended direction is the one you are moving in. Since taking a wrong turn can derail you, take time before you act by listening to yourself one more time.

Evening Reflection: My Insights from Today

May 25, _____

Mental

The needs of others may interfere with what you think is best for you.
Pay attention to your highest goals.

Spiritual

Meditation time allows you to recognize your needs.
Please yourself before you please others.

Emotional

Transform others by transforming yourself.

Physical

Your body is your beacon from which you can radiate positive energy.

Integration

Strong energy around you may push you toward precipitous actions. Stay aligned with your inner values, and make sure you listen to the expectations of others prior to making any commitment to them. You can only care for others as well as you care for yourself. Conserve your energy by making sure you have time for self-reflection and self-balancing during the day.

Evening Reflection: My Insights from Today

_____

_____

_____

_____

_____

_____

_____

_____

_____

_____

_____

May 26, _____
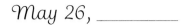

Mental
Pay special attention to self-talk, and keep it empowering.

Spiritual
Stay balanced in your *Axes of Awareness* (see resources on page 373).

Emotional
Spending time with your animals may be extremely beneficial.
"Purr" yourself.

Physical
Watch your digestion, especially when in social circles.

Integration
Conflict between your needs and those of others may come into play when you are under pressure to accomplish daily tasks. Ask, "What is most important? What are my priorities?" Stay with these first, and if you have energy to spare, then decide how you want to use that energy. Check in with yourself often to make sure you remain in balance and harmony with yourself.

Evening Reflection: My Insights from Today

May 27, _____

Mental
Utilize your skills by attending to the nuances of your ideas
so small ideas can become big ones.

Spiritual
Take time alone for realigning, rebalancing, and reorienting.

Emotional
Stay with your inner direction despite pressures around you.
Take care talking to yourself as well as to others.

Physical
Exercising when you are tired is extremely risky today.
Less is more sometimes.

Integration
Build on your strongest skills by recognizing how you use those skills throughout your day in ways you may not have considered. Notice the small things
you do such as preparing a meal, getting dressed, calling a friend. All of these
small actions require complex skills. Just notice and acknowledge. Watch
your confidence grow bigger as your recognition of small things expands.
You are more than you think you are, and you know more than you think
you know.

Evening Reflection: My Insights from Today

_____

_____

_____

_____

_____

_____

_____

_____

_____

May 28, _____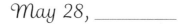

Mental

Stay focused on what is important to you so you maximize your possibilities.

Spiritual

When meditating make sure that you consider
how all layers of awareness integrate in your life.

Emotional

Consider how your feelings shift as they reflect your feelings
and the feelings of those around you.

Physical

Build stamina while recognizing the limitations
and vulnerabilities of your body.

Integration

Pay attention to the signals you receive from your body while focusing on what you want to have happen in your immediate future. When you consider moving forward toward your goals, make sure you correctly identify the tasks at hand and how you want them to play out. Be patient in mapping out your plans so you have a clear vision and sense for how you want things to play out.

Evening Reflection: My Insights from Today

May 29, ＿＿＿＿＿

Mental
Think about your social interactions and how they impact your thinking.

Spiritual
When you relate your gut responses to social interactions,
you gain self-knowledge more than knowledge about
the others involved in the interactions.

Emotional
Transformation of your behavior depends on your emotional awareness.

Physical
Subtle cues you get from your body tell you about what is healthy for you.

Integration
Getting caught up in circumstances of the day may derail you from your inner process and pull you away from what you want to do in your life. Limit your activities to those that enhance your direction in moving forward toward your goals, and listen to your inner Self. Take time away from your daily busy-ness to rebalance internally and to refresh your spirit.

Evening Reflection: My Insights from Today

May 30, _____

Mental
Recognize that struggles often have to do with seeking approval from others.

Spiritual
When you stay with what you know about yourself
and claim your inner authority, you are likely to feel empowered.

Emotional
Often wellbeing depends on self-approval rather than other people.

Physical
Health is rooted in the correct alignment of all areas of your life.

Integration
Use your empathy of the feelings of others to inform your creative visualizations of how things can align for you as well as for them. Limit your reactions and impulses until you visualize how things can move forward in best alignment or balance for all concerned. Be cautious about acting too quickly.

Evening Reflection: My Insights from Today

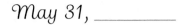

May 31, _____

Mental
Register information about yourself
and recognize that you are a work in progress.

Spiritual
Sometimes what seems like a limitation
puts you in touch with your deepest talents.

Emotional
Relationships benefit when you are honest about your deepest feelings.

Physical
Recognize what you can and cannot do, and stand
by it to assure you mitigate stress on your body.

Integration
Be mindful of ways you shift during the day. Much of your awareness is
beneath the surface of your mind, and it is only by astute observation of
yourself and your reactions that you gain clarity about the depth of your
responses. Take time during your day to listen for your inner knowing and
pay attention to the messages you receive from all levels of yourself.

Evening Reflection: My Insights from Today

_____

_____

_____

_____

_____

_____

_____

_____

_____

_____

June 1, _____

Mental
Consider what you actually know as fact before you speak or act.

Spiritual
Empower your inner process through self-recognition and self-restraint.

Emotional
Sensitivity to the emotions of others may affect your balance.

Physical
Gauge your physical stamina before you commit to taking things on.

Integration
True clarity depends on considering all possibilities prior to committing to a viewpoint. Listen to your feelings, but also consider the context of them and what you want to have happen if you act or express your perspective. Be wise and cautious before making any promises.

Evening Reflection: My Insights from Today

June 2, _____

Mental
Empowered change is possible when you learn from past experiences.

Spiritual
Recognize the depth of your intuitive Self and trust it.

Emotional
You are open and vulnerable to the feelings of others.
Stand up for what you need gently and without emotional reactivity.

Physical
Think before you take on more today physically than you are prepared for.

Integration
You gain strength today if you tune in to and tap in to your inner resources.
What do you know about your inner resources? When you use your inner
wisdom, that's like what? Be creative and courageous.

Evening Reflection: My Insights from Today

June 3, _____

Mental
Use your mind to register integrative dynamics within yourself.

Spiritual
Action aligned with your inner Self feels free of stress
and comes from deep within you.

Emotional
Being open to the emotions of others
may make you vulnerable to their wishes.

Physical
Pushing yourself physically when with others will deplete you today.

Integration
Stay focused on your deep knowing that whispers gently to you rather than listening to the reactive emotions that surface in your day to day life. Let your feelings serve you rather than the other way around. Be mindful and alert to opportunities, and let yourself flow without pushing or forcing any situations.

Evening Reflection: My Insights from Today

June 4, _____

Mental

The way you perceive those around you may impact you
more than you think. Take time to consider all options
and your inner feelings before coming to any conclusions.

Spiritual

Breathing meditations help relieve stress in your body.
Watch your breath now. Let the Divine breathe you.

Emotional

Emotional pressures from others may push you to action before you are clear.
Take time to consider consequences before you react.

Physical

Err on the side of doing less rather than more today.
You are physically vulnerable.

Integration

Allowing old outworn ways of expressing yourself to shift and change with
your new insights can move you toward greater health and wellbeing. Take
time to tap in to yourself long enough in each new situation of your day
to listen to your inner voice and pay attention to the resonant energy deep
inside you. Act from there if at all.

Evening Reflection: My Insights from Today

June 5, _____

Mental
Consider telling your "story" in a different way
or from a different perspective.

Spiritual
Keep self-clarity as a priority.
It is more crucial to your balance than collective empathy.

Emotional
Carefully visualize consequences of your actions
so you create your own destiny.

Physical
You may be likely to overextend or overexert yourself today. Be on alert.

Integration
Ongoing challenges in your life focus provide opportunities for change. Use these challenges to create new possibilities and outcomes for yourself and for others. Be creative in your thinking, and replay your story with new metaphors and images to bring about new outcomes. Knowing what you know now, what actions might you take from this space in yourself?

Evening Reflection: My Insights from Today

June 6, _____

Mental
You know yourself better than anyone knows you.
What do you know about your strengths and talents?

Spiritual
Claim your inner authority and power by trusting your perceptions.

Emotional
Careful visualization of consequences can short-circuit emotional actions.

Physical
Overexertion and overeating are a danger today.

Integration
You know your vulnerabilities and sensitivities better than anyone else. Stay focused on the direction you know is right for you despite outside input. Trust your inner guidance more than the emotional input of others. Pay attention to what you want to have happen, and limit your focus to pinpoint your first steps.

Evening Reflection: My Insights from Today

June 7, _____

Mental
Mental clarity comes and goes as your grasp of issues waxes and wanes.

Spiritual
Collective needs speak loudly and move you strongly toward action.
Take as good care of yourself as you do of others.

Emotional
Loving compassion shifts feelings and perceptions.

Physical
Physical depletion is likely if you allow yourself to be under stress.

Integration
Emotions are generally tricky to interpret because they can so easily be mis-
interpreted and acted upon in misleading ways. Stay focused on the common
thread of caring that exists in all people. Act from this place of unity and love,
and let emotional stress go.

Evening Reflection: My Insights from Today

June 8, _____

Mental
When you limit your actions to your deepest values
and use your resources appropriately, you are likely to be well-received.

Spiritual
Sensitivity makes time for processing essential. Be quiet and solitary.

Emotional
Treat others with the same compassion and
understanding you want from them.

Physical
Rest is essential. Exercise conservatively and eat with discipline.

Integration
When you function with awareness of your multidimensional nature, you
are most likely attuning yourself to your deepest core values. Check yourself
during your day to make sure you align with what you know at your deepest
level of Self. You are a divine and important being, acknowledge your inner
power to yourself, and express it kindly through your energy to others.

Evening Reflection: My Insights from Today

June 9, _____

Mental
Consider consequences before you decide
how to spend inner and outer resources.

Spiritual
Time to tune into yourself is well-spent, especially when you listen
to your inner voice of wisdom and take direction from it.

Emotional
By watching your emotional reactions, you are able to consider
how you want to relate and respond in each moment.

Physical
Notice your physical reactions, and when stressed,
pause, breathe, release tension, and rebalance your energy.

Integration
With the open energy pattern on the inner layers of consciousness today,
it is important that you keep your self-talk positive and tap into your inner
wisdom about your feelings and perceptions to stay balanced. Remembering
past ways of handling things allows you the opportunity to make new choices
in the present.

Evening Reflection: My Insights from Today

June 10, _____

Mental
Take the time you need to think in new ways. Stay positive.

Spiritual
Setting intention now allows you to manifest the future. Dream big.

Emotional
You can modify your behavior by using creative intelligence
and awareness to attain balance.

Physical
Confusion and overload mentally may put you under undue pressure.
Take time to rest.

Integration
Navigating the tricky energies challenges everyone to remain balanced despite daily frustrations and setbacks. Remember to call upon your inner resources that tap into your core resilience and divine Self. You can be sensitive, compassionate, and balanced in terms of getting your needs met if you take time to self-reflect and speak with kind honesty when you speak.

Evening Reflection: My Insights from Today

June 11, _____

Mental

When visualizing the best for yourself that you can imagine, that's like what?

Spiritual

What do you know about your creative Self now?

Emotional

Feel free to try out new roles and take on new ways of being
if they feel aligned and balanced at the depth of your being.

Physical

Energy blocks in your body cause discomfort
and bring attention to where you need to get "unstuck."
Visualize your body free of discomfort, healthy, and balanced.

Integration

When energy on the inner plane of consciousness is open and flowing, you have an opportunity to find balance in yourself that aligns you to your deep Self. Take this time to reframe your images and let go of old patterns that contain limiting beliefs.

Evening Reflection: My Insights from Today

June 12, _____

Mental
Perceptions change from moment to moment.
Remain open to all new information.

Spiritual
Taking time to consider alternative actions allows you to reflect
on how you might affect and be affected by others.

Emotional
Premature verbalizations activate tensions
when ungrounded emotions are triggered.

Physical
You can enhance your health by paying attention
to your body and its balance.

Integration
Take charge of what you want to have happen in ways that recognize and
use your inner and outer resources. Cosmic energies support alignment and
balance when you honor your intuitive Self and listen to your need for awareness on the Mental, Spiritual, Emotional, and Physical layers of functioning.
Let your life sing. It's song is unique and beautiful.

Evening Reflection: My Insights from Today

_____

_____

_____

_____

_____

_____

_____

_____

June 13,  _____

Mental
You affect others with how you handle yourself
and how you frame your questions.

Spiritual
Secure decisions are difficult today so take time to "sleep" on things.

Emotional
Consider your plans including
who will support your choices and honor them.

Physical
Move slowly and with caution to avoid overexertion and overeating.

Integration
Mental energy and limiting beliefs may blind-side you so take care to review
your choices carefully and act with caution. When you are at your best with
others, that's like what? When you are balanced, that's like what? Are you in
the right space to be balanced? If not, what needs to happen for balance to
happen?

Evening Reflection: My Insights from Today

_____

_____

_____

_____

_____

_____

_____

_____

_____

June 14, _____

Mental
Changing your story now will serve you well in the future.
Reconsider your assumptions.

Spiritual
You have many inner resources to call upon.
Take time to meditate on your strengths.

Emotional
Speak honestly from your depth of Self
and listen sensitively to the "tells" in the responses.

Physical
Exercise with caution and conserve your energetic resources
so you stay balanced and healthy.

Integration
Call upon your inner strength, and use it toward self-awareness. When you
act from a place of inner aligned strength, you are then able to use your
resources freely to benefit and be of service to others. The more you recognize yourself as a microcosm of the macrocosm and take self-responsibility,
the more you contribute to the balance and wellbeing of the whole.

Evening Reflection: My Insights from Today

June 15, _____

Mental

Speak from your depth of Self and stay true to what you know of yourself.
Watch for "tells" in yourself and others.

Spiritual

Review your perceptions from the point of view of the other person.

Emotional

Behave toward others as you want them to behave toward you.

Physical

Take plenty of time to be quiet and avoid stressful situations.

Integration

Listen beneath the surface so you hear the truth behind the words. Apply this
practice to yourself as well as to others throughout the day. Cosmic energy
patterns are likely to trigger emotional reactivity. When you recognize your
emotions but quickly return to a calm and balanced inner space, you will
know you have mastered an important step in your process.

Evening Reflection: My Insights from Today

June 16, _____

Mental
Acknowledge your accomplishments by paying attention
to ways you learned from past experiences.

Spiritual
How you connect with yourself is how you connect with others.
Take time for self-reflection and self-recognition.

Emotional
Always remember that you are a multidimensional being
who affects and is affected by what is around you.
Take time to consider consequences before you make commitments.

Physical
Your physical resources are important to your health.
Consider your energy reserves and plan accordingly.

Integration
You are a multidimensional being. When you align to your inner Self and
what you know to be balanced for you according to your highest spiritual
principles, you are most likely to feel fulfilled. Take time to tune in to yourself even when outside pressures push you toward action. Be your own best
advocate.

Evening Reflection: My Insights from Today

June 17, _____

Mental

Speak only after you consider how words you speak might be perceived.
Use your inner wisdom to monitor your speech.

Spiritual

You might question your inner process and its wisdom.
Trust that you know more than you think you know and take time
to frame your inner words positively in ways that build self-esteem.

Emotional

Be alert to taking on feelings of others before you are clear yourself.

Physical

Focus on your breathing while you move through your day.
Stay internal. Let the Divine breathe you.

Integration

Remembering experiences so you can use their lessons in the present can inform your actions positively. Take time to think through what you want to have happen and how it can happen before you commit to any action. Speak your truth with compassion and kindness. Treat others as you wish they would treat you.

Evening Reflection: My Insights from Today

June 18, _____

Mental
You may feel pressured to take action before you are internally ready.

Spiritual
Stay mindful of your inner values, and limit your attention
to those areas of your life that support those values.

Emotional
Recognize the consequences your words may have on others
and how their words affect you.

Physical
Pushing yourself physically may be depleting and unwise.

Integration
Identify and balance yourself by meditating and focusing on what is important for you before you move into the tasks of your day. Keep this focus throughout your day and return periodically during the day to check back in with yourself to make sure you are on track and moving forward toward your goals. Make adjustments so you stay balanced and in touch with your inner Self throughout the day.

Evening Reflection: My Insights from Today

June 19, _____

Mental
Information overload may confuse you and activate self-doubt.

Spiritual
Attending to what you already know works for you is important
in determining how you spend your energy.

Emotional
You are extremely open to the feelings of others
and vulnerable their opinions. Monitor emotional reactivity
and err on the side of non-response rather than impulsive actions.

Physical
Rest more than you think you need to and do less
than you think you "should."

Integration
While you can accomplish a lot, it is sometimes wise to take time to reassess
your situation and what is important. Time alone, putting your focus on your
strengths and refining your creative process can be a good use of your time.
Plan ahead and make room in your day for your own self-reflection.

Evening Reflection: My Insights from Today

June 20, _____

Mental
New options and ideas are accessible if you open your mind fully.
Use a beginner's mind and make no assumptions.

Spiritual
Wait to act until you know without any question
what your inner voice tells you.

Emotional
Allow your vision of your future to be informed by your values
and their practicality rather than by your fantasy and beliefs.

Physical
Avoid pushing your body. Eat and drink with discipline.
Rest and meditate to stay balanced.

Integration
When energy shifts consciousness, you are likely to notice shifts in your perceptions and feelings. Use the shifts of awareness you notice to realign and rebalance so you stay true to your highest values and express yourself internally and externally from that centered and balanced place of inner awareness.

Evening Reflection: My Insights from Today

June 21, _____

Mental
Watch your breathing to capture the still point
between inhalation and exhalation.

Spiritual
Shifts in your energy alert you to the depth of possibilities within.

Emotional
Social situations influence you so be patient and take your time.

Physical
Navigating the pressures on you may cause you some stress
unless you plan ways to recharge and realign.
Take time to do so in order to take care of your physical body.

Integration
Staying focused on your inner place of knowing is best achieved when you
take time alone to reset your daily priorities so you use your talents and skills
in ways that accomplish your daily goals. Remind yourself to tune in to your
"tells" regularly throughout your day to remain balanced.

Evening Reflection: My Insights from Today

June 22, _____

Mental
Some confusion about what you really think may overwhelm you.
Be patient, and take time to sort things out.

Spiritual
Tap into what you know about yourself and your sensitivities
to tune into your best way to navigate the day.
Taking time first thing in the morning will serve you by aligning you
to yourself so you can move from center throughout your day.

Emotional
You are vulnerable to the pressures on you emotionally from situations
and people around you. Take a deep breath before reacting.

Physical
You are vulnerable to pushing yourself physically to please others.

Integration
You know deeply when you are balanced and when you are in touch with
yourself. Make sure you tap into this knowing and stay alert to it throughout
your day. You are likely to be a bit tossed about by outside pressures and
emotional energy, so be prepared by finding your center early in the day.

Evening Reflection: My Insights from Today

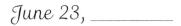

June 23, _____

Mental
You prevent missteps when you change your thoughts
and perceptions to learn from your experiences.

Spiritual
You are extremely open to others and are best served
by staying internally quiet.

Emotional
Impulsive reactions endanger your physical balance and eating patterns.

Physical
You are physically vulnerable to stress and emotions.
Use past experiences to monitor your activities.

Integration
Review the *Axes of Awareness* (see resources on page 373). Pay special attention today to the way your body "tells" and feeling "tells" inform your awareness of yourself. By recognizing what and how you process information, you gain awareness and from that awareness can take action that is meaningful and purposeful to you. Take care of yourself.

Evening Reflection: My Insights from Today

June 24, _____

Mental
Give more weight to your inner process than to your thoughts today.
Ask new questions.

Spiritual
Use your inner gut responses to inform you,
but make choices that carry the wisdom of experience with them.

Emotional
Social pressures may push you because of your sensitivity to others.

Physical
Use caution in risky situations. Conserve your energy.

Integration
Use life circumstances to provide you with information. Take this information about your inner reactions and instincts. Process your experiences with intelligence, thus taking charge of how you move forward in reaching your highest goals. Take your time, be patient.

Evening Reflection: My Insights from Today

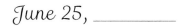

June 25, _____

Mental
Pay attention to the way you receive information.
Watch for your body to give you signals and align yourself
to what you perceive and think consciously.

Spiritual
Your inner knowing is more subtly attuned than your mind.
Listen for your inner voice to guide you during the day
and honor the alignment it guides you toward.

Emotional
Take pressure off yourself and others to make decisions or to take action.

Physical
Rest regenerates strength, while exercise may be depleting today.

Integration
Strong energy can work to strength your sense of purpose or it can work against you if you are unclear. Make sure you take charge of your inner resources and use them to build the kind of life you want. Think ahead and plan your projects carefully so they serve you well.

Evening Reflection: My Insights from Today

June 26, _____

Mental

Be prepared for surprises as you uncover new ideas.

Spiritual

Your inner sensitivities are a gift that brings you all kinds of knowledge.
Take the time to meditate and listen to your inner depth.

Emotional

Be wary about promising to do more than you can deliver.
Take on new commitments carefully and consciously.

Physical

You may feel more energy when you are with others
than when you're alone today.

Integration

You are a multidimensional being living in the Mental, Spiritual, Emotional, and Physical Worlds. It is important to recognize the vulnerabilities and strengths of each area of your life. Notice how your awareness shifts as you move through your day. Make conscious choices by keeping your balance and using your inner resources carefully.

Evening Reflection: My Insights from Today

June 27, _____

Mental

Information overload may divert your attention from your inner voice
of wisdom. Listen for it before you make assumptions
about any action you might want to take.

Spiritual

Use breathing as a way of monitoring your balance
so you trust you are taking aligned action.

Emotional

Only take action if you feel calm and unstressed.

Physical

Rest continues to be healthy. Avoid pushing yourself.

Integration

Premature action may require revision later. Stay empathic spiritually while
watching your own internal changes. Consider what heightens your perceptions of how things may play out in the future, and mull them over in the next
few weeks. Use this time to prepare for the summer with resolve to take care
of yourself.

Evening Reflection: My Insights from Today

June 28, _____

Mental
Allow information to excite your fantasies and build future dreams.

Spiritual
Deep introspection allows you to anchor your core
from a place of self-knowledge.

Emotional
Wait to take any action until you sleep on things for a night or two.

Physical
Measure your activity level based on your known physical capacity.

Integration
What is correct for other people may not be correct for you. It is essential
that you operate from a place of inner wisdom and empower yourself by
envisioning what you want to have happen and how it might best be orches-
trated in your life. Take time to review your plans and commit only to things
that move your life forward in ways that you value.

Evening Reflection: My Insights from Today

June 29, _____

Mental
Think about how you know what you know.
Sort through your mind to find areas that are most important
to you to address, and think about how you might do that.

Spiritual
Your inner process is key to your sense of balance.
Take time to meditate and recognize your deep sensitivities.

Emotional
Demands of others challenge your inner resolve to stay true to yourself.

Physical
Eat carefully and thoughtfully.

Integration
When you are functioning and living at your best, that's like what? In answering this question, pay attention to all areas of your life. Ask the question of each area of your consciousness, mentally, spiritually, emotionally, and physically, e.g., "When functioning and living at my emotional best, that's like what? When functioning and living at my physical best, that's like what?"

Evening Reflection: My Insights from Today

June 30, _____

Mental
Consider things you feel most deeply connected with, and express gratitude.

Spiritual
Rely heavily on your intuitive voice of wisdom.
Honor your inner intelligence.

Emotional
Words carry strong energy. Use them carefully and positively.
Watch your reactions to the words of others.

Physical
Setting clear limits on your physical stressors allows you
to focus and stay healthy.

Integration
Cosmic energy requires alert attention so you can differentiate the way it impacts you and others. Recognize that you always have choices and can navigate and take time and space in your day to rebalance and realign. Use physical tools to assure this happens, e.g., tapping, Tai Chi Gung, walking.

Evening Reflection: My Insights from Today

July 1, _____

Mental
Question your assumptions despite a desire to find a simple answer.

Spiritual
Remain alert to what you want to have happen for yourself
before you tune in to the needs of others.

Emotional
Take charge of your emotions rather than allowing them to drive you.

Physical
Rest and take a break from hard workouts. Eat lightly.

Integration
Staying in touch with all layers of your Self may challenge you. Make sure
to focus your attention on your breathing and if you are at all emotionally
reactive, pull back and realign your energy. It is an important time for self-
reflection so you move forward in your life in ways that reflect your inner
balance and talents.

Evening Reflection: My Insights from Today

July 2, _____

Mental
Stay firm in your resolve to take your time while you consider what you want.
Avoid jumping to conclusions.

Spiritual
Subtle whispers of gut feelings give you information.
Take your instinctive responses into contemplation in order to gain clarity.
Do not take action unless you are clear.

Emotional
New ideas about past experiences may reveal information.

Physical
Breathe with awareness. Let the Divine breathe you — breathe so quietly
that you barely know you are breathing.

Integration
Depth of awareness opens your mind to many new ideas and possibilities.
Thus, take your time before responding so you are certain that your actions
and reactions come from a clear and intentional place within. You are able
to integrate information but only after you are still and aware of different
possibilities.

Evening Reflection: My Insights from Today

July 3, _____

Mental

Choices are open to you. Define what you want to have happen
before you make any commitments.

Spiritual

Stay spiritually connected to your deepest values
by taking time alone to tune in to your inner Self.

Emotional

Protect your space and take time before you respond
to situations or people emotionally.

Physical

Digestion is sensitive today. Eat consciously.

Integration

Emotional energy often triggers physical reactions unconsciously. Be especially mindful about your physical reactions and how they inform your considered actions. Take time to feel your inner balance, and visualize how your contemplated actions may play out before you commit to any path.

Evening Reflection: My Insights from Today

July 4, _____

Mental
Allow your inner responses and awareness to guide your mind.

Spiritual
High empathy and deep sensitivity open you to others. Remain aware.

Emotional
Your viewpoint and feelings are important. Hold to what you know
is true for you despite pressure from others around you.

Physical
If you exercise or play any sports,
take into account your physical vulnerabilities.

Integration
How you think about yourself and other people impacts your reactions. Take
time to think before you speak. In addition, monitor your inner self-talk. How
you treat yourself is how you treat other people. Be kind.

Evening Reflection: My Insights from Today

July 5, _____

Mental
Allow information to excite your fantasies and build future dreams.

Spiritual
Be alert to ways you take care of yourself, recognizing
that how you care for yourself is how you care for others.

Emotional
When you react to the pressures around you,
you are vulnerable to moving away from your own balance. Be alert.

Physical
When in social situations, pay special attention to your physical vulnerabilities.
Do only what you can do easily.

Integration
Creative energy from social interactions may fuel your inspirations but can also lead you away from your inner Self. Stay alert and mindful of your inner balance so you live your own story and not the story someone else has created for you. Be as kind to yourself as you are to others.

Evening Reflection: My Insights from Today

July 6, _____

Mental
Process information fully before allowing yourself to draw conclusions.

Spiritual
Alertness to your past self-perceptions
can bring you into greater alignment now.

Emotional
Waiting for the right moment is one way to monitor your reactions
and defuse emotional misperceptions.

Physical
Rest when you are tired, despite pressure from others to push yourself.
Eat only when you're hungry.

Integration
Your intuition is likely to be triggered by circumstances in which you find yourself. Take the gentle whispers of your inner voice seriously. Take a breath and wait until you frame your perceptions carefully before speaking or reacting. Meditation will serve you well.

Evening Reflection: My Insights from Today

July 7, _____

Mental

Express empowering feelings through encouraging those you love
to reach their potential.

Spiritual

Inner alignment or balance is key to achieving your life purpose.
When in doubt about your inner harmony,
take time alone and use your intuition as a guide.

Emotional

Listen to your tone of voice. Does it accurately reflect your feelings?
Are you reflecting what you want others to perceive?

Physical

Use your body as a transmitter radiating loving light energy from your heart.

Integration

Your inner balance and depth are best expressed when you take time to listen
to your inner Self before you commit to or take any action. Wait for clarity —
the sense that you know from within — before you move forward. What do
you want to have happen?

Evening Reflection: My Insights from Today

July 8, _____

Mental
Reframe your thoughts projecting positive ideas for the coming week.

Spiritual
Notice how you feel when alone and with others.

Emotional
Limit emotional reactions by intuitive as well as mental discipline.

Physical
Set exercise goals before you begin exercising.

Integration
When you are penetrating to the depth of your awareness, that's like what? Set clear goals for yourself for the day, and remain accountable to yourself for achieving them. *Noble Energy Wellness Tools* (see resources on page 373) can help you express gratitude in all Four Worlds. By working in all the worlds, you integrate your consciousness in a way that allows it to manifest what you have envisioned.

Evening Reflection: My Insights from Today

July 9, _____

Mental
Shifting energy may heighten your sensitivities.
Avoid putting pressure on yourself.

Spiritual
Your intuitive instincts speak to you through your body. Listen.

Emotional
Remain alert to social "tells" in others.

Physical
Make sure you rest, and decide in favor of doing less rather than more.

Integration
Balance often depends on listening to your body when it gives you subtle signals. When you tune in to what your gut tells you about how to take care of your body, and you remain disciplined in that care-taking, your wellbeing is enhanced in more ways that you probably recognize. Listen for the subtle "tells" that alert you to your body/feeling/mind balance.

Evening Reflection: My Insights from Today

July 10, _____

Mental

Remain open-minded to new possibilities. Think before you speak.
Once spoken, words have energy and impact.

Spiritual

You can tap into your deepest aspirations if you take time to be alone,
and then listen for the voice deep within you
that knows because it knows.

Emotional

Emotional reactivity may move you away from what you want to have happen.
Be mindful of your reactions and monitor them carefully.

Physical

Breathe as quietly as you can. Let your breathing be so still
that you imagine you are not even breathing. Feel your presence within.

Integration

Emotional reactions can lead you away from your goals if you move too
quickly to action. Take time to listen for your inner voice, and make certain
that you align and balance the your needs of the moment with longer term
perspectives. Be cautious.

Evening Reflection: My Insights from Today

July 11, _____

Mental
Consider options open to you in your life now.
When you are excited and passionate about your goals, that's like what?

Spiritual
Own your inner power to create the life you imagine for yourself.
Be your best advocate.

Emotional
When you are most balanced and in alignment with your deepest passions,
what kind of goals are most important to you?

Physical
Doing more than you are comfortable doing may tax you physically.
Be kind to your body. Get plenty of rest.

Integration
New patterns are emerging. Use this time to reassess your goals as you consider what is most important to you in your life. Listen to all areas of your being: Mental, Spiritual, Emotional, and Physical. Use your words carefully. Listen to *Build a Strong Sense of Self* (see resources on page 373), to set new patterns in motion and to anchor positive resiliency.

Evening Reflection: My Insights from Today

July 12, _____

Mental

Conflicting signals may lead you to reconsider past assumptions.
It is a good time to move toward new possibilities.

Spiritual

Meditate. Take extra time for yourself and deepen inner awareness.

Emotional

Take a step back before taking any action.

Physical

Promises are easy to make in the context of situations,
but they may put undue pressure on you.

Integration

The depth of who you are most empowers you when you listen to and honor
your inner direction. Take time alone to rebalance your energies throughout
the day. If you feel emotional, wait until you are calm, and use your words
carefully.

Evening Reflection: My Insights from Today

_____

_____

_____

_____

_____

_____

_____

_____

_____

_____

July 13, _____

Mental
How you do anything is how you do everything.
Be mindful and careful before you take any action.

Spiritual
Self-reflection about possible paths you can take
will open you to future options.

Emotional
Impulsive verbalizations may later be regretted. Wait for clarity.

Physical
Keep your energy contained and avoid overexertion in all areas.

Integration
Focus your attention on what you want to have happen rather than on momentary irritations of your day. Recognize that when you are stressed, it is likely that those around you are stressed too. At such times, go within yourself, gain dominion over your emotions, and be kind to yourself and others. Listen to *Build a Strong Sense of Self* (see resources on page 373) to learn how to set new patterns in motion and to anchor empowered resiliency.

Evening Reflection: My Insights from Today

July 14, _____

Mental
When you speak, consider how your words
can enhance the lives of those with whom you connect.

Spiritual
It is important to stay in touch with your deepest
and highest goals when framing what you want to have happen.

Emotional
Take time to monitor your emotions within your body for stability.

Physical
Breathe as you anchor stillness within your body and balance your emotions.

Integration
Be alert to emotional reactions, and rise to the challenges they present. Stay focused on what is important to you at a level of your core values, i.e., the things you most care about and feel committed to. You are unique. Your experiences are unique. They inform your journey. Use them as you set your intention for new outcomes.

Evening Reflection: My Insights from Today

July 15, _____

Mental
Visualize goals clearly before you make any decisions
or draw any conclusions.

Spiritual
Continue to set aside alone time and meditate.
Your inner clarity depends on time alone and on recognizing inner quiet.

Emotional
Words freeze feelings. Consider how you want to be perceived.

Physical
Listening to your body requires alert discernment of your body's subtle "tells."

Integration
Stay in touch with what is most important to you in your life and put your
attention on these areas. Use your inner resources to enhance your inner
process by taking time to carefully consider your intentions and how what
you are considering as actions may play out in reality. Wait until you are
clear before taking any actions.

Evening Reflection: My Insights from Today

July 16, _____

Mental

Use *SMART Goals* (see resources on page 373) to check that your short term goals align with your longer term goals. Small steps make a difference.

Spiritual

Integrate deep inner feelings into your action plans.

Emotional

Self-criticism undermines your self-esteem.
Remain positive, and reframe negatives to positive.

Physical

Pushing yourself can deplete you on all levels. Be kind to your body.

Integration

How you use your inner resources so you honor all areas of your life is important. Take stock of your inner sense of balance and make sure that you check in with yourself during your day. It is easy to get pulled away from your focus by circumstances and people around you. Stay focused and keep your thoughts empowering to build resilience.

Evening Reflection: My Insights from Today

July 17, _____

Mental
You may have many ideas that push for answers. Patience is important in finding your own truth. Trust your need to process things your own way.

Spiritual
Meditation clears your space to recognize your own feelings and the energy of others who enter your space.

Emotional
How you treat others is how you treat yourself.

Physical
Overexercising is a risk and may be unhealthy today.

Integration
You are likely to pick up on the energies around you and may get caught up in activities that are not in line with what you value most for yourself. Take time alone to reorient and rebalance during the course of your day. Keep your priorities in focus by limiting commitments and by doing less than you think you should do. Rest when possible.

Evening Reflection: My Insights from Today

July 18, _____

Mental

Imagine telling a new friend about your life in a new way.
Reframe your experiences from a different perspective.

Spiritual

Self-empowerment gains energy when you take time to listen to your inner
instincts and discern clearly what is important to you in your life.

Emotional

Craft a new story for yourself to change what you feel.

Physical

Balance the *Axes of Awareness* (see resources on page 373),
and release stress as you do so.

Integration

Identify activities that you enjoy and that feed your soul. These are areas to
focus on in your life so you move positively toward accomplishing your life
purpose and goals. How you do anything is how you do everything. Remain
mindful that your actions and reactions move you toward what you want to
have happen in your life.

Evening Reflection: My Insights from Today

_____

_____

_____

_____

_____

_____

_____

_____

_____

July 19, _____

Mental
What you think may not always align with what you feel.
Be mindful of all layers of yourself, and take time to process information.

Spiritual
Inner recognition of your vulnerabilities carries a lot of information.

Emotional
Use your intuition to set limits on how you react to circumstances over which
you have little control. Breathe into your depth, and be still in the process.

Physical
Use your intuition to set limits on how you react to circumstances over which
you have little control. Breathe into your depth, and be still in the process.

Integration
You are likely to feel most in balance when you tune into your body signals
and register them intuitively at the deepest level of knowing. You have the
capacity to take charge over what you feel and how you express your inner
Self. Be mindful of yourself as a vehicle of consciousness, and use your intelligence in discerning truth from falsity.

Evening Reflection: My Insights from Today

July 20, _____

Mental
Consider what project you might want to begin in the next few weeks.
Many options are open to you. Wait before you make any commitments.

Spiritual
Do something that you know takes care of you today. Stay focused on this activity.

Emotional
Release any concern for what others want you to do or be.
Be yourself, and honor your feelings if your emotions are balanced.

Physical
You may pay the price later for pushing your body too much today.
Get plenty of rest, and err on the side of less rather than more.

Integration
What do you know about the laws that guide your life? What kind of boundaries are the boundaries you use to limit your space to remain clear and to keep your focus on what you know about yourself and what works for you? Listen to your inner guidance and the message it gives you.

Evening Reflection: My Insights from Today

July 21, _____

Mental

Mental pressure is likely to create some stress.
Pay attention to your self-talk. Be non-judgmental.

Spiritual

Time alone allows you to listen to your inner voice
and penetrate to the depths of your inner Self.

Emotional

Nurture those who nurture you in return.

Physical

Do only what you know is healthy. Limit your exercise to routines you know.

Integration

Limiting where and how you spend your time is crucial to your balance. Pay special attention to your fleeting thoughts, and listen for the wisdom beneath their surface. Remain focused on your inner alignment, making sure you use your inner resources on what you most value.

Evening Reflection: My Insights from Today

July 22, _____

Mental

Energy always follows thought. If you focus on the negative
from your past, you will move in a negative direction.

Spiritual

Creatively rewrite stories from your past.
Imagine their positive energy growing.

Emotional

Focus on and learn from past empowering social interactions.

Physical

You are tuned in to other people physically.
Set your own limits on what is healthy for you.

Integration

Be careful with your words so they accurately reflect your intentions. Your
mind is a powerful tool best used when you focus on empowering resources
and energy, directing it so you align your thoughts with your inner Self congruently. Ask, "What do I know about my inner resources now?"

Evening Reflection: My Insights from Today

July 23, _____

Mental
When out in the world, you have a chance to get information
that changes your perspective on things.

Spiritual
You are connected to everyone and feel it strongly today.

Emotional
The needs and desires of others may distract you from yourself.

Physical
Nonverbal physical "tells" give a lot of information
about yourself and others.

Integration
Your body is an important source of information that guides you throughout
your day. Tune into your body sensations by limiting your focus of attention
and by erring on the side of doing less rather than more. You can deplete
your energy if you focus on too many things and extend yourself too much.

Evening Reflection: My Insights from Today

July 24, _____

Mental
Time and patience are critical in gaining clarity
about your responses and what truly resonates with you.

Spiritual
Set your intention on avoiding distractions today. Use focus.

Emotional
Emotional reactions tune you in to the collective energies
around you as well as to your own feelings. Be wise in what you focus on.

Physical
Stay restful and play. Pushing your body is risky.

Integration
When you listen to your inner guidance regarding your self-direction, you
are most likely to feel an internal sense of balance. Be mindful of the way
you move away from your inner truth when around other people and when
circumstances challenge your beliefs. Stay true to yourself.

Evening Reflection: My Insights from Today

July 25, ﹍﹍﹍﹍﹍

Mental

Often the outcome you experience is in the detail
and how well you have paid attention to it.

Spiritual

Use energy techniques to shift anxieties that come up in interactions.
Let them pass. They will dissipate quickly.

Emotional

Recognize that your depth of awareness informs your choices.
Pay attention to the *Axes of Awareness* (see resources on page 373).

Physical

Exercise with discipline and attention to subtle muscle movements.

Integration

Envision what you want, and set your intention on accomplishing it over
time. It takes time for intentions to manifest in reality, giving you feedback
so you can correct misperceptions and reapportion your inner and outer
resources. Make use of time as a precious gift.

Evening Reflection: My Insights from Today

July 26, _____

Mental
Return to issues you want to figure out and understand.

Spiritual
Review your internal dialogues, and listen deeply to what you tell yourself.

Emotional
Put emotions aside and allow them to settle for a few days.
Err on the side of silence rather than speaking impulsively.

Physical
Watch what your body tells you and use your intelligence
in interpreting the information.

Integration
You know more than you think you know and naturally align to signals your
body gives you. Your body is one of your best feedback systems guiding you
along your true path. What do you know about your body balance now?

Evening Reflection: My Insights from Today

July 27, _____

Mental
Take in all the information you receive, but make no judgment.

Spiritual
You are so tuned in to others it is important to pay
special attention to how you take care of yourself.

Emotional
Put your emotions aside for now and let them settle for a few days.

Physical
Relax but remain cautious about exercise and eating.
You may feel pushed and challenged by others.

Integration
Learning from past experiences about your sensitivities informs your choices
and gives you good feedback about where and how to monitor your energy.
Use your intelligence to stay balanced even when you are challenged and
reactive. Use words carefully and responsibly.

Evening Reflection: My Insights from Today

July 28, _____

Mental
Pay attention to small details. They can help you enormously.

Spiritual
Trust what you know about yourself.
Inner balance and harmony are critical to how you operate in the world.

Emotional
Your feelings may be affected by others in ways you will regret later.

Physical
Eat very cautiously when in social situations. Be disciplined.

Integration
Your mind is a powerful tool that you can use to monitor your reactions so
you honor your deepest Self and live in accord with your highest purpose.
When you are in doubt or unclear, wait. Meditate so you focus on your inner
space and rebalance to your highest Self.

Evening Reflection: My Insights from Today

July 29, _____

Mental
Speaking prematurely about your ideas may concretize
them before you have them fleshed out.

Spiritual
Pressures from the day may challenge you to focus on yourself
and what you need. Take time to meditate, and stay with your inner guidance.

Emotional
Words have power to mobilize emotions. Use them with care.

Physical
Watch your eating patterns and breathing patterns for signs of social stress.

Integration
Communication is crucial to framing your self-esteem. Be as kind to yourself
as you are to others, and be gentle with how you say what you feel. Self-talk
builds resilience. What does your body tell you that aligns with you today and
what do you want to have happen for yourself?

Evening Reflection: My Insights from Today

July 30, _____

Mental
Change your thinking to change your feelings.
Your mind is a powerful source of change. Use its intelligence in creative ways.

Spiritual
The *Axes of Awareness* (see resources on page 373) and its balance
is important in keeping you aligned.

Emotional
You are highly sensitive to the energies of the day. Be mindful of your reactions
and whether they resonate with what you know about yourself.

Physical
Patience before making commitments protects your health.

Integration
Cosmic energies flow through you constantly, shifting your focus and feelings
as they move through your cells. Listen for your depth of Self by being mindful
of subtle cues that you receive about what you know about what you know.
When you know at a depth of certainty what is right for you, stay true to it.

Evening Reflection: My Insights from Today

July 31, _____

Mental
Questioning yourself and considering
all possible options open to you is healthy.

Spiritual
Your consciousness is important because you are a microcosm
of the macrocosm. Be the best you can be, and stand up for yourself.

Emotional
Inner gut responses are hard to pin down, so be loving
and patient with yourself and with others.

Physical
Be very gentle with your body today and avoid pushing it.

Integration
You are a multidimensional being. At times it is tricky to recognize all worlds
and to balance them in yourself. Be patient with yourself and with others and
ask yourself, "Am I in the right space? Am I in right alignment? What do I
know about my inner space now?"

Evening Reflection: My Insights from Today

August 1, _____

Mental
Pay attention to thoughts because you have answers
to what you want to know.

Spiritual
Indecision is healthy today. Let it be.

Emotional
Notice things in the environment that influence you.

Physical
Allowing others to push you when you need rest is risky.

Integration
When you pay attention to the subtle signals your body gives you as you move through your day, you might notice that memories activate in you. These memories connect stories of your life to current situations from which you can learn important lessons. Use your mind to focus on what is important and what you know. With all you know now, what do you want to have happen?

Evening Reflection: My Insights from Today

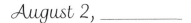

August 2, _____

Mental
Mental overload may distract you from what is important.
Take time to review assumptions. Ask new questions.

Spiritual
Meditation time can be a time of inner activity followed by quiet.
Your depth of awareness informs you in multiple ways.
Listen for the voice of understanding and knowing.

Emotional
Connections to other people can influence your feelings
and pressure you in ways that create internal stress.
Pay attention to yourself and be honest with others.

Physical
Get plenty of rest.

Integration
Your immune system is sensitive to the influences around you in ways that
affect you on all levels of awareness. When you set your intention to use your
energetic resources carefully and well, you take dominion over your fleeting
desires and can make clear choices. What kinds of choices are the choices
before you now?

Evening Reflection: My Insights from Today

August 3, _____

Mental
Remain open-minded when considering the way things and people affect you.

Spiritual
Take meditative time today, by yourself, to check and reorient your direction.
Call upon past experiences to gauge whether you need
to adjust your perspectives.

Emotional
You are emotionally vulnerable to the pushes and pulls of others.

Physical
Quiet time is most healthy today.

Integration
Awareness and love often require that you have the courage to stand up to what you know is aligned with you. When you take action that honors all components of yourself, you are likely to experience more love of yourself and you'll probably notice that this love radiates to others as well. What kind of things in your life now require courage of honoring yourself over others?

Evening Reflection: My Insights from Today

August 4, _____

Mental
Take time to think before you speak.
Be certain you know what you want to say.

Spiritual
When you envision your life as you ideally want it to be, it's like what?

Emotional
When you notice emotional reactivity, ask yourself
if expressing your emotions aligns with your desired outcome?

Physical
Pushing your body may compromise your health.

Integration
The ebb and flow of cosmic energy can shift your perspective. Use this time to
clarify what you want to have happen and what happens when that happens.
Doubts and fears are natural until you gain the wisdom and understanding
to discern choices with true clarity. You are in process. Trust your process
and listen to your inner voice.

Evening Reflection: My Insights from Today

August 5, _____

Mental
Avoid situations you would rather avoid.

Spiritual
Stay with what you know works for you and stay quiet when possible.

Emotional
Note situations that affect your eating and watch what you eat.

Physical
Your body is your friend. Ask it for advice and listen to what it says.

Integration
It is an important time to tune in to your deepest remembrance of core principles that guide your life. When balanced and in touch with your true Self, that's like what? Take time to remember times when you felt most yourself. Luxuriate in those memories, and send them loving energy for their reminders.

Evening Reflection: My Insights from Today

_____

_____

_____

_____

_____

_____

_____

_____

_____

_____

_____

August 6, _____

Mental
Consider new information you may not have previously considered.

Spiritual
Make sure you take time to meditate in your own private space.

Emotional
Emotions of others impact you. Take time to tune into
your physical body to discern what feelings belong to you.

Physical
You are a very finely tuned instrument. Listen to its music.

Integration
You can only do what your body allows you to do. Listen to its voice carefully
and thoroughly consider the risks you take and how you want to manifest
what you know. Internal process carries the power of intention. Use it well.

Evening Reflection: My Insights from Today

August 7, _____

Mental
Avoid mental overload by remaining alert and focused on your tasks at hand.

Spiritual
Find inner strength to follow what you know works for you in your life.

Emotional
Pressures from others and from the environment may pull you away from yourself. Speak with caution, especially about emotional issues.

Physical
Stay quiet. Eat and exercise with care. Listen to body signals.

Integration
Compassion for the needs of others may pull you away from yourself. Be extremely discerning about your direction and commit only to those things that have the highest probability of helping you realize your deepest Self. Be wary of spending your resources, including energetic ones, on things you may not truly value.

Evening Reflection: My Insights from Today

August 8, _____

Mental
Use your creative intelligence to balance the
body/instinct/mind and feeling/instinct/mind parts of yourself.

Spiritual
You are part of a wider collective. Everyone is linked in consciousness.
Take time to tap into your awareness.

Emotional
Keep emotional reactions in check
and make sure you use your mind to monitor your feelings.

Physical
Stay tuned in to what your body tells you. It is very wise.

Integration
Remembering yourself and what you want to have happen in your life is critical to putting your energy in the right space. Ask what you know from this space in yourself and your life now. Are you in the right space? Facing in the right direction? Is your perspective right? What do you know now from this space here?

Evening Reflection: My Insights from Today

August 9, _____

Mental
Open your mind to new possibilities
and avoid narrowing yourself in the process.

Spiritual
Inner balance requires self-reflective monitoring
and mindful responses to others.

Emotional
Emotional friction is a high probability if you express yourself impulsively.

Physical
Use your body as your antennae
and receive subtle signals from what is around you.

Integration
Taking charge of your emotions and what you want to have happen through your responses is a big step in achieving balance. Change your responses and assumptions to change yourself and the outcomes in your life. Keep a long view instead of a short one.

Evening Reflection: My Insights from Today

August 10, _____

Mental
Use past self-knowledge to make current judgments,
but remain flexible in perspective.

Spiritual
Time alone in meditation is time very well spent.
Align to your deepest Self and avoid conflicts that stress you physically.

Emotional
Moods of others may affect your mood. Be on alert.

Physical
Health is key to balance. Use your energy wisely today.

Integration
Mental pressure may activate your thoughts in unexpected directions. Be on
alert for saying the wrong thing in the wrong place for what you intend. Tune
in to your memories of past times when you were in tune with yourself, and
use this knowledge and understanding to inform your current choices.

Evening Reflection: My Insights from Today

August 11, _____

Mental
When you consider all perspectives, consider your assumptions
beneath your ideas and reconsider possibilities.

Spiritual
Be alert for your inner voice of wisdom that tells you about yourself.

Emotional
Recognizing what you feel and how it impacts you
is essential to gaining mastery over your emotional reactions.

Physical
Rest is essential and likely to be elusive when pressures from others play upon
you. Take care of your health by protecting your energy.

Integration
How you balance the *Axes of Awareness* (see resources on page 373) i.e., your
body/instinct mind and feeling/instinct/mind, impacts how you experience
yourself and the world. Take time to assess your balance and make sure that
you are clear about your goals and that they are *SMART goals* (see resources
on page 373).

Evening Reflection: My Insights from Today

August 12, _____

Mental

Take stock of things that you might want to improve in your life.
De-clutter your mind as well as your environment.

Spiritual

Stay tuned to ways you can nurture yourself so you remain in balance.

Emotional

Recognize when others influence your feelings and you shift
to accommodate them.

Physical

Eating according to what you know is good for your body,
especially when you are around others.

Integration

Explaining away your deepest intuitions can create stress and confusion for you. Take stock of what you want to have happen and how you want it to happen. Set your intentions clearly and be ready to adapt and adjust when what you thought you intended plays out differently. This is the way you learn and rise to challenges that push you toward clarity.

Evening Reflection: My Insights from Today

August 13, _____

Mental
Pay attention to how you frame your thoughts.
The questions are more essential than your answers.

Spiritual
Be certain to take plenty of meditation time today.

Emotional
Pressures from others may pull away from your own feelings. Be on alert.

Physical
Avoid crowds and all overindulgences.

Integration
When you are most sensitive to the energies of others and to cosmic tensions, it is wise to limit your interactive field so you can handle the unexpected and find balance in the moment. Throughout the day, stop periodically from what you are doing and ask, "What do I now know? What do I want to have happen now?"

Evening Reflection: My Insights from Today

August 14, 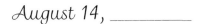 _____

Mental

Mental pressures may push you to speak before you fully formulate your thoughts. Be patient, and when in doubt, be silent.

Spiritual

Take time for yourself. It is essential today.

Emotional

Download and listen to, *Build a Strong Sense of Self* (see resources on page 373). It can shift you and your day.

Physical

Your body is how you receive information. Take care of it lovingly.

Integration

Self-Recognition requires that you take an honest look at yourself and your sensitivities and back away from commitments that no longer serve your life. Take care of yourself as you take care of others. Be as kind and caring to yourself as you would be to those you love most deeply.

Evening Reflection: My Insights from Today

August 15, _____

Mental
Observe your mental process without judgment while you wait for clarity.

Spiritual
Time to meditate is essential in reorienting your perspective
and anchoring your instincts.

Emotional
You avoid social pressure when you stay in tune with your
deepest feelings and listen to yourself first.

Physical
Overdoing any activity puts you under undue pressure today.

Integration
A single standard is important when considering balance in your life. How
you do anything is how you do everything. How you use and balance your
inner resources reflects on how you balance your resources in the world. Be
mindful and use one guiding standard for balance.

Evening Reflection: My Insights from Today

August 16, _____

Mental
Conflicting messages from your body and feelings may confuse you.

Spiritual
Trust your inner intuitive guidance. It always speaks the truth to you.

Emotional
Impulsive emotional reactions may put you at greater risk today.

Physical
Use your breathing to monitor your stress.
Breathe as though the Divine breathes you.

Integration
Speaking before you are clear may commit you prematurely to a direction that you may later wish to revise. Before you speak, recognize that understanding comes before words. The nuances of words reflect depth and experience in balance when you exercise caution by waiting for true discerning clarity.

Evening Reflection: My Insights from Today

August 17, _____

Mental

Open energy may put you on overload. Be mindful of your sensitivities and rely on past experiences to inform current situations.

Spiritual

Meditation time is essential. It empowers you in ways that allow you to reach your highest potential with authenticity.

Emotional

What others want may be at odds with your true needs, wants, and desires.

Physical

Your body is your friend. Use it with wisdom and with care.

Integration

Emotional recognition and discerning where you want to place yourself in the energy of emotion impacts your balance in any situation. Be wise in your use of your energy and carefully consider how you want to orient yourself now. Ask, "Is there a space I can move to now from which I can be more clear?"

Evening Reflection: My Insights from Today

August 18, _____

Mental
Consider the source of your information before you draw any conclusions.

Spiritual
Be sure to take time for yourself today.
Only through this inner process is alignment possible.

Emotional
How you feel in your body tells you a lot about your emotions.

Physical
Your health and its balance is essential for the foundation of your future.

Integration
What does your source of information want to have happen? Does this align
with what you want to have happen based on your wisdom and knowledge?

Evening Reflection: My Insights from Today

August 19, _____

Mental

Reality provides information and questions. Answers come in their own way.

Spiritual

When you sleep you become one with the consciousness of the totality.
Be responsible by attuning yourself.

Emotional

Transform your emotions to set an example for others.

Physical

When you feel healthy, it is easier to balance your emotions.
Take time to settle into your body.

Integration

How you use your energetic resources helps balance your ability to manifest what is truly possible. When you visualize what you want for yourself, be mindful of limiting it to what is possible and realistic. *SMART goals* (see resources on page 373) are important because they build a foundation upon which you move forward. Listen to yourself carefully and adjust accordingly.

Evening Reflection: My Insights from Today

August 20, _____

Mental

Limit your higher mind to refrain from over-expansion.

Spiritual

Meditate to balance and to assure your feelings
are in sync with your deepest Self.

Emotional

Emotional reactivity is best monitored when you are with others.

Physical

Eat cautiously and avoid overexercising.

Integration

Sensitivity to others may activate old feelings in you. Stay in tune with what
you know about yourself and your deepest Self. Take time alone to meditate
and do something nurturing for yourself. Make sure you are balanced and in
touch with your Mental, Spiritual, Emotional, and Physical Selves.

Evening Reflection: My Insights from Today

August 21, _____

Mental

Allow yourself to expand the limits of your consciousness,
but be cautious before drawing any conclusions.

Spiritual

Meditation time is important. Use it to tap into the quiet still place deep
within you. You are free of distortion from others in that place.
Go there and ask, "What do I know from this quiet still place inside me?"

Emotional

Conserve emotional resources. Put boundaries on what you promise.

Physical

It is important to use discipline on how you eat
and how you spend your energy.

Integration

Sensitivity to others and to the collective consciousness of which you are a
part are likely to pull you away from yourself. Take time to be internal and to
find where that still knowing inside yourself is.

Evening Reflection: My Insights from Today

_____

_____

_____

_____

_____

_____

_____

_____

_____

_____

_____

August 22, _____

Mental
What you are thinking and mulling over is best kept private for now.

Spiritual
Listen for the inner whispers of yourself.
You may be guided by questions you may wish to avoid answering.

Emotional
It may be tricky to recognize when other people influence what you feel.

Physical
You may release tension if you exercise in moderation today.

Integration
Before you commit to any action, be certain that the outcomes of your action align congruently with your intended goals. You are vulnerable to the energy of others and can be diverted easily from your own Self. Be mindful of how sensitive you are.

Evening Reflection: My Insights from Today

August 23, _____

Mental
Action for the sake of action may result in more risk than necessary.

Spiritual
Self-care is always essential before you can attend properly to others.
When in doubt, wait it out.

Emotional
Many modalities trigger intuitive knowing.
Listen for emotional reactions as well as inner whispers,
and learn to discern differences on how you receive information.

Physical
Take no physical risks today.

Integration
Taking action because you can is not always wise. Make certain that you have taken time to consider the implications and consequences of your contemplated actions before you commit to a direction. You choose your path. Take dominion.

Evening Reflection: My Insights from Today

August 24, _____

Mental
Past "puzzle" pieces of your life may suddenly become clearer to you.

Spiritual
Discovering your inner purpose and voice is essential in staying true to your life path. Own your inner power and let it guide you.

Emotional
Vulnerabilities to emotions of others push you. Keep on alert in this respect.

Physical
Your health depends on discerning what is healthy or unhealthy for you in particular. Pay attention to your body and listen to its "tells."

Integration
Recognition of your depth and skill in discerning what is true and what is not can lead you toward mastery. Be mindful of your inner balance and use it as a guide in considering possible paths for yourself. Err on the side of inaction rather than on the side of action.

Evening Reflection: My Insights from Today

August 25, _____

Mental

Dissonance between outside and internal pressures may put you in conflict.
Learn from past mistakes.

Spiritual

Before taking any action, take some quiet meditative time
for self-analysis of your contemplated path.

Emotional

Avoid social commitments that go against what you know you want.

Physical

Breathe with awareness to remain unstressed.

Integration

Be mindful of any unconscious pulls toward gaining approval of others. Any
action you contemplate is best served if it is free from a need for approval or
from a want for control. Ask if you are free of these emotional nuances when
considering your choices.

Evening Reflection: My Insights from Today

_____

_____

_____

_____

_____

_____

_____

_____

_____

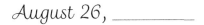

August 26, _____

Mental
Quiet time quiets your mind and allows new ideas.

Spiritual
Your purpose in service of a wider collective
may become clearer to you today. Take time to meditate.

Emotional
Avoid social commitments that go against what you know you want.

Physical
Doing too much physically may take a toll on you energetically.
Balance rest with activity.

Integration
The stories you tell yourself about your life focus your energy. Change your
stories to change your life. Notice and replay events in your life as you put
your mind on new ways you could have or might have responded that would
have changed the outcome of your interpretation of the events and/or people.
Realign with a new outcome, and watch as your life shifts in focus.

Evening Reflection: My Insights from Today

August 27, _____

Mental
Quiet time quiets your mind and allows new ideas.

Spiritual
You live in Four Worlds. Each world has an element associated with it.
Pay attention to the four elements,
fire, earth, air, and water, in your environment.

Emotional
What do you love doing and how does that align
with what you are doing now in your life?

Physical
Your body is vulnerable when you are around other people.
Pay attention, and be disciplined when out socially.

Integration
You are a unique individual here to manifest in your own way. Being true to
yourself requires that you honor your individuality and own it in your own
way. Have the courage to be yourself. What do you know about yourself now?

Evening Reflection: My Insights from Today

_____

_____

_____

_____

_____

_____

_____

_____

_____

August 28, _____

Mental
The opinions and stories of those around you may influence your thinking. Make no assumptions, and remain open to new possibilities.

Spiritual
Rest and activity are essential in staying meditatively balanced.

Emotional
Overextending yourself to others may put pressure on you emotionally.

Physical
Stress is likely if you take on too much physically.

Integration
Your spiritual purpose in life is essential to your sense that you are realizing your fullest potential. Be mindful of the flame that ignites your passions especially if they are free of outside influences.

Evening Reflection: My Insights from Today

August 29, _____

Mental
When planning for the future, consider your talents
as well as your depth of purpose.

Spiritual
Trust that you know deep within what you need.

Emotional
Meeting new people may open new vistas for you.

Physical
Digestion is touchy today. Eat and exercise with extreme care.

Integration
Doubt about your vision for your own future may surface when you take
in more information that you need, especially if others fuel your doubts.
Take time to assess your resources energetically, and plan to use them well.
You can achieve your goals when you allocate your internal and external
resources carefully and claim your inner authority.

Evening Reflection: My Insights from Today

August 30, 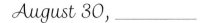 _____

Mental
Allow your mind to receive possibilities that open doors within you.

Spiritual
Time alone builds internal connectedness as it aligns and renews you.

Emotional
When in social situations, be on alert for pressures
that pull you away from yourself and your needs.

Physical
Pay special attention to your digestive needs.
Avoid exercise if at all strenuous.

Integration
Collective needs and pressures may pull you away from what you know is important for you at this time. This distraction from your own process may divert you from realizing your goals over the next few months. Be mindful of staying balanced, and consider the consequence over time of choices you make now.

Evening Reflection: My Insights from Today

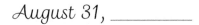

August 31, _____

Mental
When you recognize the higher purpose in what you choose,
you are able to understand more than you can verbalize.

Spiritual
When you feel balanced, you are aligned with your highest Self.

Emotional
Make sure you transform emotional reactions before you take any action.

Physical
Energy follows thought. Visualize a healthy body.

Integration
Before you take any action, consider the way your reactions and feelings
balance through all layers of yourself: Mental, Spiritual, Emotional, and
Physical. If you envision that what you want to have happen can happen in
the way you are visualizing it realistically, then commit to your path and trust
that it will happen. But, be clear about your facts and discern them with the
courage of honesty.

Evening Reflection: My Insights from Today

_____

_____

_____

_____

_____

_____

_____

_____

_____

_____

_____

September 1, _____

Mental

Stay alert for ways you deny what you know
because you would rather perceive in old ways.

Spiritual

When your vision carries personal responsibility and accountability,
your outcome has its best chance of success.

Emotional

Take time to recognize ways you can balance your emotions.
Act only when you are in alignment.

Physical

Make certain that you exercise only as much as feels healthy for your body. Eat
only foods that you know feel good to your body when you eat them.

Integration

In order to manifest what you want to have happen, it is essential to base
your assumptions on facts and reality rather than on beliefs about possibilities. Plan ahead by aligning your inner wisdom and understanding with what
you know is true, and be discerning in your assessments.

Evening Reflection: My Insights from Today

September 2, _____

Mental
Reconsidering past assumptions and basing your thinking
in fact is important in moving forward.

Spiritual
Listen for the whisper of your intuitive voice that informs you
of the link between your mind and your body.

Emotional
Reinterpretations of past relationships may help you grow.

Physical
Health depends on letting go of past "dis-ease" in all areas of yourself.

Integration
Listening to your body signals and what they tell you about your relationships
is especially productive when you remain open-minded to new possibilities.
You know more than you think you know and can align with new ways of
thinking if you clarify what you want to have happen and how it can happen.

Evening Reflection: My Insights from Today

September 3, _____

Mental
Let your imagination soar, but stay grounded at the same time.

Spiritual
Tune in to the depth of your intuitive Self,
and check in with your inner sense of balance throughout the day.

Emotional
Promising more than you want to deliver is risky emotionally.

Physical
Monitor how you spend your energy because you are vulnerable
to overindulgence and overexertion today.

Integration
Balancing the *Axes of Awareness* (see resources on page 373), i.e., the body/
instinct/mind and feeling/instinct/mind, is crucial to recognizing how you
are influenced by circumstances and pressures around you. Stay quiet when
you feel pressured by outside elements. Take time to meditate and be quiet
when overloaded.

Evening Reflection: My Insights from Today

September 4, _____

Mental
Ideas may begin to formulate,
and you may be able to verbalize them internally.

Spiritual
Your intuitive awareness may gain momentum when you take time alone
and focus on how you want to relate to people and circumstances in your life.

Emotional
Self-refinement of emotions is essential for depth and grounding.

Physical
Err on the side of rest rather than activity. When in doubt, rest.

Integration
Before jumping into action in any way, take time to consider what you want to
have happen and how you want to relate to others in the process. Who else is
involved in what you are planning? Are you emotionally balanced? When you
know what you want to have happen, then what needs to happen?

Evening Reflection: My Insights from Today

September 5, _____

Mental

True empowerment comes from having the courage to stand up
for what you know is right despite the opinions of those around you.

Spiritual

Meditation time is critical for balance and for tuning in to your deepest Self.

Emotional

Change yourself to change your life. Your are your own best teacher.

Physical

When you walk, notice how you breathe. Pay attention, in a relaxed way,
to gain the most information about this pattern.

Integration

You function in multiple layers of awareness simultaneously. Sometimes it
is difficult to discern what you want and how your energy bodies interface
within you. Listen to your body carefully so you hear the whispers it gives
you about your energy levels and inner resources. Budget your energy as
carefully as you budget your money.

Evening Reflection: My Insights from Today

September 6, _____

Mental

What you tell yourself may or may not be true. Keep an open beginner's mind when interacting in the world. Assume nothing and be open to change.

Spiritual

Awakening to vibrational harmony takes time, patience, and courage.

Emotional

When those around you are emotional, you are likely to feel what they feel.

Physical

Watch your breathing for signs of stress.
Take your time, and remain aware of your body. Feel your toes.
Feel your head. Now feel your body in between your toes and head.

Integration

When you recognize the acute sensitivity of your body to receive signals that impact you beneath your level of awareness, you are better able to tune in to those signals and make them conscious. Once conscious, you have the ability to use your understanding to grasp new possibilities for your future. Take time to be alone, meditate, and rebalance in the course of your day.

Evening Reflection: My Insights from Today

September 7, _____

Mental
You generally know more than you think you know. Listen to your intuition.

Spiritual
Spiritual self-fulfillment empowers you in ways
that reverberate to those around you. Be your best Self.

Emotional
How you care for yourself is essential. Remain true to what you
already know about yourself and stay with your known goals.

Physical
You are vulnerable to physical depletion
and overload today. Get plenty of rest.

Integration
How you do anything is how you do everything. Take your time when moving through your day. Avoid rushing or pushing through things because you experience pressures from outside yourself. Make sure you use your known talents and wisdom as you move forward through your day.

Evening Reflection: My Insights from Today

September 8, _____

Mental

Dominion means that your higher Self monitors what your instincts tell you. Err on the side of inaction and reconsider your assumptions.

Spiritual

Resolve to take charge of your life, and wait respectfully, for clarity.

Emotional

Review lessons learned over the past few weeks.

Physical

Pay attention to your inner physical alignment. Notice how you feel when your body aligns properly and when you move with awareness.

Integration

Using your mind to accurately discern fact from belief is essential in gaining clarity and consciousness. Examine your goals using the same critical eye you would use if those goals were not yours. Be ruthless in seeking truth and in dispelling misperceptions.

Evening Reflection: My Insights from Today

_____

_____

_____

_____

_____

_____

_____

_____

_____

_____

September 9, _____

Mental
What you already know about yourself is key in recognizing
what feels in tune with what you want.

Spiritual
Those closest to you whom you can trust recognize
your sensitivities and sensibilities.

Emotional
Emotional stress regarding relationships may carry strong messages about what
you need, want, and desire for better alignment.

Physical
Pay attention to what your body needs.
Listen to your body as well as your mind.

Integration
What do you know about the way people in your life impact you physically?
When at your most balanced, mentally, spiritually, emotionally, and physically, that's like what? And what do you know now about what needs to happen for balance to happen?

Evening Reflection: My Insights from Today

_____

_____

_____

_____

_____

_____

_____

_____

_____

September 10, _____

Mental

Because you are open to the feelings of others,
you may need time alone to realign and rebalance yourself.

Spiritual

Take time away from the activities of your day to listen for your inner wisdom
and to make sure you are aligned to your inner process.

Emotional

Emotional stress regarding relationships may carry strong messages about what
you need, want, and desire for better alignment.

Physical

Your body "tells" are crucial in guiding you toward balance.

Integration

Envisioning what you want to have happen is important in setting your intention clearly for manifestation. However, remember that the manifestation process takes three full months to unfold. During this time, input from others and from your doubting Self may distort your process. Be on alert to your inner guidance system for rebalancing your intentions, and keep them clear.

Evening Reflection: My Insights from Today

_____

_____

_____

_____

_____

_____

_____

_____

September 11, _____

Mental
Check that you feel in charge of your choices in life.

Spiritual
Vulnerability to the desires of others makes time alone
especially important today.

Emotional
You are likely to feel emotional when others are around.
Be protective and err on the side of silence.

Physical
Eat carefully when around others and be disciplined
with what you know about your body.

Integration
Remaining aware of the limitations of your physical energy allows you to plan
how you want to spend your time and energy. Such planning is essential in
moving forward toward your goals. Start your day with some time/energy
management strategies so your day unfolds in a balanced and fluid way.

Evening Reflection: My Insights from Today

September 12, _____

Mental
Take time to consider past associations to present circumstances
for useful information.

Spiritual
You remain very tuned in to others. Let them tune in to you also.

Emotional
Emotional volatility is a danger from outside pressures.

Physical
Overeating and overexertion is a significant danger today.

Integration
Before taking any actions, it is always wise to consider if you are internally in
an aligned or balanced space. Time alone allows you to consider all perspectives and to assure that you are operating from your highest Self. This is key
to manifesting what your true intentions are.

Evening Reflection: My Insights from Today

September 13, _____

Mental
Past questions about shifts in relationships may be answered.

Spiritual
How you approach communication can make a difference in the outcome.

Emotional
Impulsive words can hurt.
Deep reflective words, when well communicated, may inform and elucidate.

Physical
Your inner instincts may be shaky.
Trust only what you know for sure about your body, and get plenty of rest.

Integration
Desires based on emotional reactions and physical attraction may be misleading. Take time to reflect on past patterns, and consider how you use your inner resources. Are your interpretations about current situations and people in your life valid? What do you know about your relationships now?

Evening Reflection: My Insights from Today

September 14, _____

Mental

What is said may not always be congruent with what is done.
Be mindful of committing only to what you really want to do.

Spiritual

Using your energy to enhance your inner awareness is energy well spent.
Take time alone to gain clarity.

Emotional

Precipitous action may cause you regret.

Physical

Be careful with your body in all respects.
You are physically vulnerable today.

Integration

Committing to more than you can accomplish is frustrating for you and for others. Consider the time and energy you need to manifest your goals realistically. Use *SMART Goals* (see resources on page 373) and work with them in the Four Worlds to gain clarity and congruity in manifesting them.

Evening Reflection: My Insights from Today

September 15, _____

Mental
Believing what you want to believe
rather than what the data shows may lead to frustration.

Spiritual
You are deeply sensitive to other people. Take time alone.

Emotional
Balancing your emotions requires self-discipline.
Use your acquired skills artfully and mindfully.

Physical
Cues from your body about your levels of stress may be monitored
through your breathing. Breathe as though the Divine is breathing you.

Integration
It is impossible to satisfy everyone all of the time. Be honest in what you say
you can and will do, and make no promises that compromise your relationship with yourself. Being honest and true to yourself is essential to having
successful honest relationships with other people.

Evening Reflection: My Insights from Today

September 16, _____

Mental
Watch your breathing for signs of mental overload and stress.

Spiritual
Your intuitive depth is your friend. Listen very closely for its wisdom.

Emotional
Your empathy for how others feel may pull you away from yourself.

Physical
Use a quick energy tool such as tapping to align yourself during the day.

Integration
Past experiences inform the present only when you process the information without distorting it by wishful interpretations. Be ready to change yourself to change your experiences rather than expecting others to change. Stay in touch with all parts of your consciousness, even the subtlest layers.

Evening Reflection: My Insights from Today

September 17, _____

Mental
Your mind is your friend. Use the information it provides.

Spiritual
When you are alone you are less influenced by the needs of others
than when you are in the company of other people.
Take time alone to connect with your true desires.

Emotional
Watch your words to assure they reflect your deepest feelings.

Physical
When you overextend yourself physically
you are likely to feel unbalanced emotionally.

Integration
Use discriminative thought to sort through your feelings, especially when you
are alone, and determine how you want to allocate your energy resources to
achieve your goals. Make choices that honor your deep intuitive Self and lead
you closer to your goals.

Evening Reflection: My Insights from Today

September 18, _____

Mental

You may be influenced by the feelings of others
and modify your thinking to please them. Be on alert for this pattern.

Spiritual

How you think about yourself is a function of your self-affirmation.
Be as care-taking of yourself as you are of others.

Emotional

When you are emotional, look at what you can learn and transform.

Physical

When you are with other people you may feel more energy
than when you are alone.

Integration

Life always moves toward balance. What works in your life shows you where
you are balanced and what does not work shows you where you are challenged toward greater balance and awareness. Consider what in your life
works and what does not. What insights might inform you about new choices
that may change things for you?

Evening Reflection: My Insights from Today

September 19, _____

Mental

Life challenges push you to think in new ways. Allow new possibilities.

Spiritual

Listen for your inner voice that connects past experiences
with present awareness. Be patient.

Emotional

Avoid impulsive emotional outbursts.
Transform emotions through intelligence.

Physical

Pushing yourself is unhealthy.

Integration

Apply what you know to your life in ways that bring about changes that lead
you closer to your goals. Inner harmony and awareness are powerful forces
driving you toward fulfillment. Let yourself experience the fullness of your
consciousness by taking alone time to meditate, and while doing so, express
gratitude for your body, mind, spirit, and emotions.

Evening Reflection: My Insights from Today

September 20, _____

Mental
Information overload and a desire to grasp more understanding
is a natural part of life.

Spiritual
Meditation and sleep renew you.
They put you in touch with deep parts of yourself.

Emotional
You are likely to sense what others feel intuitively today. Pay attention.

Physical
Your body has intelligence beyond what you can begin to comprehend.
It is a perfect machine.

Integration
When you use your mind to discern correctly for yourself, your life flows
naturally and effortlessly. What do you know now about your life purpose?
Are you going in the right direction? Are you in the right space? Are you
aligned to your talents and passions? Now what do you know about yourself?

Evening Reflection: My Insights from Today

September 21, _____

Mental
Visualize the possibilities of realizing your dreams.

Spiritual
Take seriously what your intuitive inner voice tells you. It is to be trusted.

Emotional
If you are unclear in any way, avoid taking action.

Physical
Physical overindulgence in all areas is a danger. Avoid risk-taking.

Integration
Inner determination can result in powerful accomplishments if you use your energy in a balanced way that respects your talents and depth. Make sure you use your energy in ways that align with your depth of Self and honors your deepest values.

Evening Reflection: My Insights from Today

September 22, _____

Mental
Look beyond the obvious to find new questions that lead to new answers.

Spiritual
Preventing missteps by listening to inner wisdom is part of growth.

Emotional
Other people who pressure you in ways
that take you away from yourself are best avoided.

Physical
Physical overindulgence in all areas is a danger. Avoid risk-taking.

Integration
You understand a great deal more than you can put into words or than you know consciously. When you take time to meditate, the worlds below the surface of your awareness activate in you and inform you in ways beyond words. Take extra time to listen to this inner wisdom today, and let it guide you as you move through your day.

Evening Reflection: My Insights from Today

September 23, _____

Mental
Past experiences tell you a lot about what you perceive.

Spiritual
Recognizing what you know about yourself anchors it in awareness.

Emotional
Allow your inner core expression instead of modifying
your feelings to please others.

Physical
You know more about your body and its needs than anyone else.
Be protective, and set an eating program in motion.

Integration
Challenges of the day carry lessons for learning if you attend to your reactions and transform them before you respond emotionally. Be certain before you speak or act that your reactions are based on reality and not illusion. Be prepared for twists and turns that create nuanced challenges to your perceptions.

Evening Reflection: My Insights from Today

September 24, _____

Mental
Review ideas during this time to check them for viability and practicality.

Spiritual
Time you take for yourself is time very well spent.

Emotional
Self-discipline is essential for your emotional health.

Physical
Pressure to act may stress you physically. Take time to breathe.

Integration
Vulnerability to the collective energy and feelings of others may pull you away from yourself. Remember what is important to you and use self-discipline to stay on your own course. Remember you are unique and important in the consciousness of the whole. Self-responsibility and accountability is key to success in all you want to accomplish.

Evening Reflection: My Insights from Today

September 25, _____

Mental
New ways of thinking are beginning to take form.
Allow them time to germinate internally.

Spiritual
Self-honesty often requires deep self-reflection and a willingness to change.

Emotional
When others influence your responses,
you are likely to move away from your unique alignment.

Physical
Body responses are instinctive
but require intelligence for proper interpretation.

Integration
Put emphasis on synthesizing what you know about yourself and your life so you have a bird's eye perspective on yourself. What do you know now about your life purpose? When you are living in balance, that's like what?

Evening Reflection: My Insights from Today

September 26, _____

Mental
Live by what you know is important in your life
rather than by any outside guide.

Spiritual
Listen to your inner responses as well as to your deep Self.

Emotional
Take time to allow emotions to settle comfortably inside yourself before
expressing them.

Physical
Overworking or overexercising carries risks to your health.

Integration
Remaining true to yourself sometimes challenges you to stand up for yourself
despite the apparent needs of others. At times, things are not as they seem.
When you recognize that your alignment and balance is one with that of
others, you can discern more accurately what needs are real and what needs
are momentary. Stay with what endures over time.

Evening Reflection: My Insights from Today

September 27, _____

Mental
Be wise and courageous in your unique point of view.

Spiritual
Vulnerability is also sensitivity to others.
Stay with what you know about yourself.

Emotional
Stay away from all emotional confrontations today.

Physical
Get plenty of rest. It is very important.

Integration
Balancing the *Axes of Awareness* (see resources on page 373) may be tricky if you are unclear about what you want to have happen and about your needs. Take time to take care of yourself so you operate in the world and with others from a place of internal balance and harmony. When in doubt, wait for clarity. Trust in your knowing what you don't know.

Evening Reflection: My Insights from Today

September 28, _____

Mental
Inner alignment is key in how you think.

Spiritual
Align to your own needs before helping others.

Emotional
You are extremely sensitive to the needs of others. Stay balanced.

Physical
Use your energy to monitor your alignment.
If you feel tired, stop, rest, and meditate.

Integration
Cosmic energy sets the tone of each day by its shifting patterns in much the way your energy shifts internally and chemically. As you work toward balance in your life, watch your words carefully. Listen for metaphors you use. They point you toward clarity in understanding the assumptions behind your words. Change your language and you change your thinking.

Evening Reflection: My Insights from Today

September 29, _____

Mental

What you know to be true becomes true when it plays out
in proper alignment. Watch for "tells."

Spiritual

Time alone is a gift that you deserve.

Emotional

Words are best not spoken today.

Physical

Eat carefully and get plenty of rest.

Integration

Be mindful of how you are impacted by the energy around you and by what
people say. Be ready to shift your ideas when what you assumed to be true
is better modified. Remember that reality shifts with your perception. Stay
focused on your inner harmony and the rest follows.

Evening Reflection: My Insights from Today

September 30, _____

Mental
Recognizing how you ask questions is the first step
in achieving clarity of thought.

Spiritual
Inner wisdom that aligns to your highest Self
gives you confidence when you need it.

Emotional
Listen to your inner feelings rather than the feelings of others.

Physical
Health depends on responding to things you know work for you.

Integration
Consider how what you are thinking might play out in reality before you commit to any action. What is important now? How do you want to spend your resources? Are you where you want to be now?

Evening Reflection: My Insights from Today

October 1, _____

Mental
Pay attention to the way you think about things.
Consider new ways of thinking.

Spiritual
Twists and turns in life often bring gifts of awareness.

Emotional
Stay connected to your inner Self rather than reacting to circumstances.

Physical
Avoid physical exertion. It is easy to overdo things today.

Integration
Allowing emotional reactions to color your perceptions can distort facts. In order to remain balanced and aligned, use your intuitive acuteness and sense of inner harmony to make certain that you are aligned to your highest Self. Pause regularly to recognize that duality is part of life and that finding your still point within is essential to finding outer balance. Use a quick tool to rebalance.

Evening Reflection: My Insights from Today

October 2, _____

Mental

Things are not always as they seem. Use both energetic and cognitive signals to consider assumptions you are making that may or may not be true.

Spiritual

You perceive and know more than you realize consciously.
Listen to your inner voice that whispers softly to you. Honor its message.

Emotional

Balance your emotions before you jump to conclusions.

Physical

Health depends on balancing rest and activity.
Be mindful about your physical resources.

Integration

You live in Four Worlds: Mental, Spiritual, Emotional, and Physical. By paying attention to your inner balance, you are able to consciously align to goals that are important to you and chose which things in your day you want to put emphasis on. Acting in haste may have negative repercussions.

Evening Reflection: My Insights from Today

October 3, _____

Mental

You are likely to be open and vulnerable to the thoughts of others.
Pay attention.

Spiritual

Take extra time alone today. It is a wonderful day to tune in to your depth.

Emotional

Emotions of others may disturb your balance.
Use your internal discipline and take dominion over your emotions.

Physical

Stay with what you know works for your body and avoid trying new things.

Integration

You may find yourself reactive to others and taking authority that is not aligned with your inner core. Take a few moments to gather your thoughts and emotions before you speak. Pay special attention to the *Axes of Awareness* (see resources on page 373).

Evening Reflection: My Insights from Today

October 4, _____

Mental
Identify issues that are important to you. They help you plan for the future.

Spiritual
What matters to you over time is more crucial than acting in the moment. Take time for self-reflection.

Emotional
You sense what others need and want.
Let them take responsibility for themselves.

Physical
You are vulnerable to depleting yourself. Take it easy.

Integration
It is sometimes tricky to stay tuned in to the balance between your inner Self and how you manifest in the world. Take time to be alone and breathe as though the Divine breathes you so you realign to your inner harmony and relate to others throughout the day from this centered place. It will serve you very well today.

Evening Reflection: My Insights from Today

October 5, _____

Mental
Recognition of the roles you play
and how you are perceived in them is important.

Spiritual
Time alone is always important before you talk about deep feelings.
Be clear with yourself first.

Emotional
Identify who "owns" a problem before you speak up.

Physical
Health is a balance between body/instinct/mind and feeling/instinct/mind. Find
a balance in yourself before taking action in any direction.

Integration
Your core values are "deal-breakers" in aligning with others in your life.
Instead of trying to force any issues, consider caring for yourself as you wish
others cared for themselves. Be the example of what you value and live it. Be
your own best Self.

Evening Reflection: My Insights from Today

October 6, _____

Mental

Remain open to inner core reactions that surface during your day.
They communicate new information to you.
Reflect on your reactions to benefit from your challenges.

Spiritual

Alignment requires self-reflection.

Emotional

Be guided by your depth of self-knowledge more than by emotions today.

Physical

Rest as much as you can today. Eat with care.

Integration

You are highly sensitive to the collective consciousness of the whole today
and may find that the energies of the day challenge your balance. Stay tuned
in to the Four Worlds: Mental, Spiritual, Emotional, and Physical, you are
more likely to be in touch with the parts of yourself that you may lose perspective of. Any reactivity is likely to cause you and others stress.

Evening Reflection: My Insights from Today

_____

_____

_____

_____

_____

_____

_____

_____

_____

_____

_____

_____

October 7, _____

Mental
Speaking before you are clear about your feelings is risky.

Spiritual
Penetrate the veil of outer illusion
and enter the world where you feel harmony within.

Emotional
You are highly vulnerable and sensitive to others.
Take charge of your emotions and keep them in check.

Physical
Use great discipline in eating today,
especially if it is an area in which you are vulnerable.

Integration
Envisioning what you want to have happen is a great tool in gaining clarity
and balance. Stay true to your inner values and when in doubt, stay quiet
and meditative so you balance and align to your true depth of Self. Truth
enhances your path, while self-deception sets up challenges for you to meet
in the course of your daily life.

Evening Reflection: My Insights from Today

October 8, _____

Mental
Radiate compassion and love to others
and remember to keep your words to yourself.

Spiritual
Intuition is a good guide when it honors what you know is true
to your long-term goals.

Emotional
Situations likely to trigger you emotionally require that you keep a level head
and stay true to your core values and goals.

Physical
Overexertion is a risk when you are ambivalent about doing something.

Integration
Strong pressures from those around you may go against what you know to
be true for yourself. Be wary of shifting your goals to please others and/or
to gain their approval. You are your best advocate and know yourself better
than anyone else. Align to your highest Self.

Evening Reflection: My Insights from Today

October 9, _____

Mental
Consider your inner resources
and perceptions that color how you think about things.

Spiritual
Inner wisdom is key to honoring yourself and achieving what you want
to have happen in your life. Take time for self-reflection.

Emotional
Depend on your wisdom in using emotional resources
and conserve your energy.

Physical
Conserve your energy since you may tend to overdo things today.

Integration
Staying in touch with your highest Self is key to meeting challenges of the day.
By operating from your center, you are likely to shift perspective in ways that
readjust to circumstances and maintain your flow, so you ultimately reach
the goals you set for yourself.

Evening Reflection: My Insights from Today

October 10, _____

Mental
Think about what you want to accomplish, and make plans for the future.

Spiritual
Watch for "tells" that give you information about your intuition
and what resonates deeply within.

Emotional
You are emotionally vulnerable to others today. Be aware.

Physical
Avoid overexertion and overindulging.

Integration
Although you may find yourself in tune on the inner plane, you may also find
yourself challenged by circumstances and reactive to them in familiar ways.
Be mindful and alert to your own reactions, and change them based on past
experiences in ways that can serve you currently.

Evening Reflection: My Insights from Today

October 11, _____

Mental
Sometimes it takes time for you to understand
what you are struggling with in your life. Be patient.

Spiritual
Your depth of creative insight is setting you in motion for the future.
Trust your process.

Emotional
Use your heightened sensitivity to others to build inner awareness.
Instead of reacting impulsively, creatively transform feelings.

Physical
Be very careful with what you eat today.

Integration
Emotional reactivity may conflict with what you want to have happen on
the deeper level of yourself. Pay attention to your "tells" so you congruently
reflect in reality what you value and what you know to be true about yourself.
Your wisdom can guide you only if you listen for your quiet inner voice that
whispers gently to you.

Evening Reflection: My Insights from Today

October 12, _____

Mental
Mental pressure may overload you with information.
Take time to just allow it to take root.

Spiritual
Inner wisdom and depth of inner purpose is ideal in enhancing your health.
Take time to meditate.

Emotional
Remember to remain disciplined despite emotions of the moment.

Physical
Physical health is best protected and enhanced by quiet time today.

Integration
Staying in touch with your inner process and goals is important in keeping centered. Stay true to your inner values, and recognize that how you care for yourself is likely to be a reflection of your self-perception. Take time to be alone, and note three things that you feel good about in terms of your accomplishments. Also note what attitude or perspective helped you succeed.

Evening Reflection: My Insights from Today

_____

_____

_____

_____

_____

_____

_____

_____

October 13, _____

Mental

Consider what you want to have happen in the future for yourself.
What do you know now about where you are in your process?

Spiritual

Stay sensitive to the alignment of your inner process.
It is what keeps you in balance.

Emotional

You are open to the emotions of others. Be strong in your sense of yourself.

Physical

Your stress level tells you if you are in the place of inner calm.
Make sure you stay in that calm still self-place today. Conserve your energy.

Integration

Mental pressure may push you in ways that create stress. Only take action if
you are certain about your path and know that action is well grounded. If you
are doubtful about taking action, wait and balance internally.

Evening Reflection: My Insights from Today

Mental

Self-deception may be high today so be wary of precipitous action.

Spiritual

Tapping into your intuition is important to keep you on track
and aligned with your inner core.

Emotional

You are highly vulnerable to the emotions of others.
Wait for the right timing in your life and in expression.

Physical

You are likely to be stressed by mixed feelings and responses today.
Take things in stride.

Integration

Strong reactions and impatience with yourself and others may create unnecessary stress. Err on the side of quiet and do less than you want to do so you have time to meditate and rebalance. Limit your activities and be mindful of whether you are heading in the right direction.

Evening Reflection: My Insights from Today

_____

_____

_____

_____

_____

_____

_____

_____

_____

_____

_____

_____

_____

October 15, _____

Mental
Taking action at this time may lead you astray.
Wait until you feel inner certainty.

Spiritual
Stay aligned in all areas of your life by listening
to your inner guiding voice of wisdom.

Emotional
Make sure you are in touch with the *Axes of Awareness* (see resources
on page 373), and review it in the reports.

Physical
Get plenty of rest. Use your breath to "check in" with how your body feels.

Integration
Use your senses to guide your intuition, and make sure you listen well to what
your inner voice tells you. Any impulsive actions are risky and can lead you
away rather than toward your goals. Be mindful of your deepest sensibilities
and honor them.

Evening Reflection: My Insights from Today

October 16, _____

Mental
Insights you have been seeking may surface today,
giving you a boost of confidence.

Spiritual
Use your intuitive self-knowledge to anchor your goals positively.

Emotional
Write down your insights about relationships and how they affect you.
Be strong in your resolve to create your world as you know it can be.

Physical
Take time to exercise. It builds strength physically and emotionally.

Integration
When you are in tune with your physical body and how you care for it, you
are likely to strengthen your core and feel aligned internally. Use your depth
of self-knowledge to identify what matters to you and how you want to use
your energy to accomplish your goals.

Evening Reflection: My Insights from Today

October 17, _____

Mental
Let your imagination take flight and play with possibilities.

Spiritual
Limit and conserve your inner resources
by taking time to tune in to your intuitive nature.

Emotional
Influences of others may lead you in the wrong direction for yourself.

Physical
Overexercising or undisciplined eating may compromise your health.
Avoid risks.

Integration
Staying in touch with your values and how you want to express them in your life is important. Spend time considering how past experiences have informed your current life circumstances. Acknowledging the wisdom of your choices and how challenges helped your growth can be amazingly freeing.

Evening Reflection: My Insights from Today

October 18, _____

Mental
Use intelligence when making decisions based on feelings.
Make sure they align with healthy choices.

Spiritual
Sometimes you are prone to changing your viewpoint to please others.
Stay true to your inner direction.

Emotional
You are open and vulnerable to the feelings of others.
Be alert, and set your intention to remain balanced.

Physical
Health depends on integrating all areas of your life. Listen to your body.

Integration
Shifting energies result in stress if you are unclear within yourself about your values, needs, and wants. Take the time to anchor yourself internally before you venture out in the world today. Listen to your body for its nonverbal "tells" and honor what it tells you.

Evening Reflection: My Insights from Today

October 19, _____

Mental
Finding ways to balance your thinking about things
is often trickier than expected.

Spiritual
When you attend to your inner process,
how you relate in the world becomes easier.

Emotional
You may feel especially sensitive to the demands of others.
Be sensitive to your inner balance and vulnerabilities. Stay disciplined.

Physical
Stay firm in your inner responses
and what you know about yourself as a way to feel less stress.

Integration
Because you are a multidimensional being, it is essential that you recognize
how and when your consciousness shifts during the day and how it varies
in different situations. Be especially mindful of different messages from
different parts of yourself, and listen to your inner Self rather than being
pressured by outside forces.

Evening Reflection: My Insights from Today

October 20, _____

Mental
Think about ways you can change important areas in your life.

Spiritual
Stay in tune with your inner depth.

Emotional
Tune in to the tension around you
and how you want to position yourself emotionally.

Physical
Look for physical "tells" that may reveal what you really feel and value.

Integration
Your depth of understanding and inner wisdom is triggered by circumstances and people who challenge your worldview. Pull back from making promises or commitments that may later put you under pressure. Use your inner resources to anchor your values and keep your focus on what is important to you.

Evening Reflection: My Insights from Today

October 21, _____

Mental
In what ways can reframing your story about yourself
open new possibilities in your life?

Spiritual
Stay firmly anchored in what you know rings true for you.

Emotional
The feelings and desires of others influence how you feel
whether you are aware of those influences or not.

Physical
Monitor your activities to balance activity and rest.
This balance is important to health today.

Integration
Words carry energy. Let your body inform you about what you know and
about what you want to have happen in the now. Be alert and mindful as
you watch for what resonates deep within yourself. Take time for yourself to
be clear about your goals and how you frame them to yourself in words. Be
specific and empowering in your self-talk.

Evening Reflection: My Insights from Today

October 22, _____

Mental
Mine the depths of what you know about yourself
to remember what fuels your passions.

Spiritual
Listen to the way you talk to yourself
and restate any language that misaligns to your goals.

Emotional
The balance between your body/instinct/mind
and feelings/instinct/mind requires self-reflective recognition
of what aligns to your highest goals. Pay attention.

Physical
Pushing your body when you are tired is counterproductive to your health.
Be gentle on your body.

Integration
Integrating all parts of yourself requires that you carefully and impartially
assess your desires to determine if your thinking and contemplated actions
align with facts and with your long term goals. Be diligent in your consideration, and use what you already know about yourself to inform your choices.

Evening Reflection: My Insights from Today

October 23, _____

Mental
Mental pressure may place you under stress. Be wary of precipitous action based on what you want rather than what is grounded in reality.

Spiritual
Make sure you take time alone to meditate.
You know yourself better than others know you.

Emotional
If you feel emotional, check if those emotions belong to you or to those around you.

Physical
A tendency to push your body is high.
Be aware, and make sure to get some rest.

Integration
The assumptions you make about the world around you influence your perceptions and interpretations. Reconsider your story, and consider other ways of orienting yourself, i.e., take a different perspective and note what happens then. What do you know now?

Evening Reflection: My Insights from Today

October 24, _____

Mental
Recognize the importance of what you project into the future in defining the way it manifests. Pay attention to details.

Spiritual
You are vulnerable to the feelings of others. Balance requires time to assess your own feelings while you find your center of alignment.

Emotional
Honor your emotions by staying true to your values.

Physical
Overexercising today may put you at risk. Eat carefully and with discipline.

Integration
What you want to happen can and will happen if you align on all layers of your consciousness. The deep intention you set on an unconscious level plays out in order to bring your awareness to it. In this way you have an opportunity to rise to the challenges of your personality and transcend them. Be courageous. Confront your challenges and be the most you can be.

Evening Reflection: My Insights from Today

_____

_____

_____

_____

_____

_____

_____

_____

_____

_____

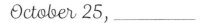

October 25, _____

Mental

External factors may put a lot of pressure on you mentally.
Think outside the box, i.e., outside what is "politically correct."

Spiritual

Depth of awareness depends on deep inner recognition
of what honors your gut.

Emotional

Stay true to the principles you hold most dear.
Keep your eye on the long-term picture.

Physical

Stay true to the principles you hold most dear.
Keep your eye on the long-term picture.

Integration

Words carry energy and once spoken cannot be unspoken. Be careful in your
words to yourself as well as to others. Judgment is positive when it corrects
misperceptions and negative when it diminishes you or others. Use judgment
as a way to align to your highest Self patiently and with compassion for your
process and the challenges you face.

Evening Reflection: My Insights from Today

October 26, _____

Mental

Pay attention to details in situations, especially in terms of their long-term consequences. What is beneath the surface is often most important.

Spiritual

Align yourself early in the day by balancing your plans
to accommodate all areas that are important to you.

Emotional

Take action if it is aligned with your inner values
and moves you closer to your long term goals.

Physical

Your intuitive sense about your body is usually worth listening to.
Listen to "tells."

Integration

When you listen to the signals that you receive from all layers of yourself, you are able to take aligned action that honors your depth of purpose and highest Self. Check in with yourself frequently during your day to assure that you are centered and balanced. Listen to *Build a Strong Sense of Self* (see resources on page 373), if you have not already done so.

Evening Reflection: My Insights from Today

October 27, _____

Mental
Take care to balance creative energy and intuition today.
Some new ideas may surface when you least expect them to do so.

Spiritual
Remain open to new ways of relating to others and to new ways of
perceiving yourself. You may have some surprises in store.

Emotional
Pay attention to how other people's emotions affect
your feelings and thoughts.

Physical
You are vulnerable to the energies around you. Rest more than you
think you need to, and err on the side of rest rather than activity.

Integration
Limiting your activities to those you know you want to do and with those with
whom you want to do them will serve you well. The balance between your
body/instinct/mind and feeling/instinct/mind is tricky and requires that you
stay alert to your own center and instincts and listen to your intuition for
guidance.

Evening Reflection: My Insights from Today

October 28, _____

Mental
Strong outside energy may push you.
Make sure your thinking aligns with what you want to have happen.

Spiritual
Anxiety is often a signal to stop and wait for clarity. Heed this signal.

Emotional
Go to the depth of your feelings and make sure fear does not drive you.

Physical
Physical sensitivity is the way your body gives you information.
Use this information wisely.

Integration
Envisioning what you want to have happen is key in getting what you actually want. Stop often during your day to check in with yourself, rebalance your energy, and make certain you are thinking clearly. Realign and readjust as situations change and as you shift perspective. You are dynamic. Live that way.

Evening Reflection: My Insights from Today

October 29, _____

Mental

When considering your path forward,
what kind of risks are the risks you might consider taking to live your dream?

Spiritual

What do you know now about the shifts you can make internally
to care for yourself better?

Emotional

People trigger feelings.
Be cautious about getting pulled into someone else's emotions.

Physical

Strength comes from within. Keep it in reserve for another day.
Rest and relax.

Integration

What kind of changes can you make in your life now to move forward toward
your goals? Is there an action from this place in your awareness now that you
can take toward living your dream? Commit to it now internally and visualize
it happening.

Evening Reflection: My Insights from Today

October 30, _____

Mental

In order to find answers, your questions must be clearly asked.
Often the question is more important than the answer.

Spiritual

Focus in meditation on how your life activities move you
closer toward your goals.

Emotional

Notice how others in your environment and life affect your emotions.

Physical

Conserve your energy for things that really matter to you.
Take care of your body.

Integration

Because you are a multidimensional being, it is important to consider all
layers of alignment before you commit to any path. Stay balanced, and take
extra internal time to meditate so you stay in touch with your deepest Self.

Evening Reflection: My Insights from Today

October 31, _____

Mental
Information overload may be confusing. Consider all options openly.

Spiritual
Focus on one thing at a time paying special attention to your body
and its responses.

Emotional
When you are emotional, notice what you are responding to.

Physical
Take time to take care of your body,
and use your senses to give you information.

Integration
When you tune in to the environment around you, what kind of perceptions
are the perceptions that get activated? What do you know about your values
and how you align with your self-care as you relate to different people?

Evening Reflection: My Insights from Today

November 1, _____

Mental
Use your senses to sort out and decipher information
that jogs your memory for clarity of understanding and interpretations.

Spiritual
Pay attention to the way you feel when you are alone compared to when you're
around other people. Take time to meditate when you are alone.

Emotional
Listen to what your gut tells you instead of how things appear.
Avoid allowing emotions to rule your actions.

Physical
Promises may put you under pressure when you are tired.

Integration
Stay tuned in to your body's signals so you "listen" to yourself on all layers
of your being. Although you live in multiple dimensions simultaneously, you
are likely to be aware of only one dimension at a time. Consequently, it is
important to take a moment here and there throughout your day to stop
whatever you are doing so you stay in touch with your deep Self and listen
for its wisdom.

Evening Reflection: My Insights from Today

November 2, _____

Mental
Inner responsibility is best focused through deep inner reflection
rather than through mental analysis.

Spiritual
Listen to and trust your inner voice. It tells you how you truly feel.
Honor your inner guidance.

Emotional
Pressure from others may undermine what is right for you.
Stay with what you know, keep your emotions to yourself, and trust yourself.

Physical
You are physically vulnerable. Pay close attention to your body.
Avoid overexertion and overeating.

Integration
Using your imagination to visualize actions you are considering can save you
from missteps. Set your goals, write them down, and make yourself accountable to someone other than just yourself. When you are accountable for
reaching your goals, you are much more likely to do so.

Evening Reflection: My Insights from Today

November 3, _____

Mental
Despite the tendency to think in "old" ways,
try making new assumptions so you gain a new outlook.

Spiritual
Trust only what you feel internally at a deep level of your inner Self.

Emotional
Balancing the *Axes of Awareness* (see resources on page 373) may be
challenging. Breathe deeply, take a few moments to center, align,
and call upon your highest Self's emotional intelligence.

Physical
Let physical sensitivity guide you toward doing
only what enhances your health. Err on the side of less rather than more.

Integration
Your physical sensitivity is a wonderful way to guide yourself toward balance.
When you listen to the "tells" of your body, and when you learn to read the
signals accurately, you are able to know when to take action that aligns with
your inner Self and when to wait for a time that is more internally aligned
with your values. Stay true to yourself.

Evening Reflection: My Insights from Today

_____

_____

_____

_____

_____

_____

_____

_____

November 4, _____

Mental
Mental pressure may push you in directions that you later regret.
Consider all options.

Spiritual
Survival often depends on following your gut response and your own path.

Emotional
Pay attention to how you feel when you are around other people.
You are likely to pick up on their feelings.

Physical
Know your physical limitations, and take them into account.

Integration
Pressures from your day may influence you. Use your inner instincts as a trigger for your remembered wisdom, and pay attention to the alignment of current attitudes and actions to your long-term goals and visions in your life. Do what you love and love what you do.

Evening Reflection: My Insights from Today

November 5, _____

Mental

Recognize that your viewpoint may vary from that of those around you. Base conclusions on your own experiences. Claim your inner authority.

Spiritual

Stay focused on your life and how you can take care of yourself. You are responsible for your own destiny.

Emotional

Tap in to your senses and adjust your emotions to balance your body.

Physical

You are physically vulnerable to the stress around you today. Be alert and aware.

Integration

A key question to ask yourself is always, "What do I want to have happen?" Being clear about what you want to have happen and then using your inner and outer resources to achieve your goals empowers you at a deep level. Be courageous, and stand up for what you know to be true about yourself.

Evening Reflection: My Insights from Today

November 6, _____

Mental
Take in and absorb all the information you can assimilate and
allow it to take root deep inside you. Wait before you draw any conclusions.

Spiritual
How you present yourself to others is a big part of how you are perceived
and perceive yourself. Be creative. Take time for yourself.

Emotional
Stay tuned in to your instincts that align your emotions
with your reactions and relationships.

Physical
Rest is crucial. You are likely to feel depleted if you do too much.

Integration
Past experiences inform you in the now. Before you take any action, or
respond emotionally in any situation, consider what you know to be fact,
and compare it to what you believe to be true. To the degree that you deceive
yourself with beliefs rather than facts, you are vulnerable to missteps and
may have to refine future actions.

Evening Reflection: My Insights from Today

November 7, _____

Mental
Keep your values in mind when you contemplate
communicating what you feel.

Spiritual
Take extra quiet time to meditate by yourself.
It is a time for patience and rest.

Emotional
Aligning your priorities is most important
in considering future directions you might take.

Physical
You may think you can do more than is healthy to do today.
Get plenty of rest if you can.

Integration
Focus on what you know about your life purpose and your next steps in moving toward achieving it in your life. With a clear direction mapped out for yourself, momentary and challenging shifts in energy are less likely to take you away from your core purpose.

Evening Reflection: My Insights from Today

_____

_____

_____

_____

_____

_____

_____

_____

_____

_____

November 8, _____

Mental
Action is possible and well conceived if you are sure
your action aligns with your values and goals.

Spiritual
Stay true to your values even if you have to shift gears.

Emotional
You sense what others feel. Be wary when you feel emotionally reactive.

Physical
Stay focused on your health, and pace yourself and your energy.

Integration
In order to have self-knowledge, you must recognize that you function on
multiple levels of consciousness. Throughout your day, it is essential to manifest your highest expression of yourself in your thinking, in your underlying
intentionality, in your emotional expression, and in how you care for your
physical body. You are in a body to awaken to your highest purpose and to
live it fully. What do you know about your highest purpose now? And when
you know, whereabouts in you is that knowing?

Evening Reflection: My Insights from Today

November 9, _____

Mental

Even when you are clear about your goals, it is wise to take each step cautiously along your path. Watch for new opportunities for new thinking.

Spiritual

Past experiences may apply to your current perceptions.
Use these memories to project positive components of them to your goals.

Emotional

Let go of ideas and feelings that no longer align with your values.

Physical

Balance by paying attention to your breathing,
and use it for monitoring your stress levels.

Integration

When nuances of focus shift your perceptions, what adjustments do you make in your attitude and perceptions to honor those shifts? Meditate on this question today. It is key to self-awareness and to utilizing the energies of the day to maximize your inner resources. Take action only if you are certain of what you want to have happen and that the outcome you want is likely.

Evening Reflection: My Insights from Today

November 10, _____

Mental

High energy and stress may pressure you toward premature action.
Exert mental discipline when interpreting situations.

Spiritual

High energetic vulnerability calls for extra self-care
and sensitivity to your need for quiet space.

Emotional

Tension is likely to come from things over which you have no control.
Promise less than you think you can deliver to reduce stress
on yourself and others.

Physical

Empowered thinking helps you stay healthy.

Integration

Make certain that you have time to yourself throughout the day to realign and rebalance your energy. Use a quick energy-enhancing tool such as tapping. Meditation is key to returning to your core Self and staying in touch with the choices you make in your life. Each moment moves you toward clarity, even when you are in the midst of challenges. Stay alert and in tune with your inner Self.

Evening Reflection: My Insights from Today

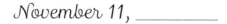

Mental

Recognize how reviewing updated information
helps you discern new ways of thinking.

Spiritual

You are likely to feel a bit afloat. Be patient,
and meditate to gain inner perspective.

Emotional

Inner alignment depends on recognition of your sensitivity
and connections with other people.

Physical

Pay attention to the interpretations you place on yourself
when you feel things in your body.

Integration

The *Axes of Awareness* (see resources on page 373) connect and balance you
as you meet new situations in their different nuances. Be on alert to how
others impact you during your day and listen for the inner voice of wisdom
that always informs you about your highest goals. If you have not yet read the
Michael Ray book, *The Highest Goal*, I highly recommend it.

Evening Reflection: My Insights from Today

November 12, _____

Mental
Watch for "tells" in yourself and others
and as a way to monitor what you choose to speak about.

Spiritual
Gaining clarity is essential in setting your future direction.
Be patient while you tune in to yourself.

Emotional
Emotional impatience can undermine you in many ways.

Physical
When you push yourself too quickly to act, you compromise your health.

Integration
As a unique individual, you interpret the world around you in your own way.
Communicating your perceptions without attachment to the impact you have
on other people may put you at risk. Tap in to your unique skills and talents
and make the most of them.

Evening Reflection: My Insights from Today

November 13, _____

Mental
Creative thinking serves you well today.

Spiritual
When you use your creative vision to imagine change
for the positive in your life, you transmit your attitude to others.

Emotional
Gratitude felt deep within your core radiates to others
and communicates to them without words.

Physical
Your intuitive sensitivity is likely to guide you well
if you listen carefully to the "tells" it sends your body.

Integration
Creative thinking and energy serve you well today. Rely on what you know
about what works for you and stay true to your highest goals. Use your mind
to oversee your reactions by deferring to your intuitive Self instead of making
assumptions that may lead you in the "wrong" direction.

Evening Reflection: My Insights from Today

November 14, _____

Mental

Taking care of things that have been waiting for your attention
is a good use of your energy today.

Spiritual

Follow your instincts to act on what you know
while appreciating that you also need rest to balance activity.

Emotional

Avoid emotionally volatile situations by identifying
where and with whom you want to spend time.

Physical

Social situations are likely to pull you away from what you know
is best for you unless you remain mindful of your limitations.

Integration

Being open to what is around you allows you to consider new ways of handling challenges in your life. Be mindful of how that has served you in the past so you can realign in the present and learn from your past. What you want to have happen can and will happen. Be aware of your inner intentions so you choose your path consciously.

Evening Reflection: My Insights from Today

November 15, _____

Mental
Action today may result in a positive outcome
if you follow through on something you feel confident about.

Spiritual
Check that your contemplated action is something you want to do
and feel sure about, i.e., make it a priority in all actions.

Emotional
Be alert to pressure from others that move you away from yourself.
Stay true to your inner Self.

Physical
Rest periodically throughout the day, even if only for a few minutes at a time.
Keep tabs on your energy, and stay alert.

Integration
How you think is very much a reflection of your inner process. Listen to *Build a Strong Sense of Self* (see resources on page 373). The foundation on which you base your choices is key to your achieving your life destiny and purpose. Make sure you have strong instincts that take you in the direction you truly want to go.

Evening Reflection: My Insights from Today

_____

_____

_____

_____

_____

_____

_____

_____

November 16, _____

Mental

What you think might "work" only works
when it follows your inner as well as outer path.

Spiritual

Tune in to your deepest core rather than telling yourself
what you want to believe to be true.

Emotional

You are open to others and may find yourself out of sync with other people.

Physical

Pushing yourself beyond your physical limits is risky.

Integration

So much of oneself often comes in response to those people who are most important to them. Take the time today to impact those you most care about by letting them know how much they mean to you, and express gratitude to them about how they have made a difference in your life. By recognizing the strengths in others, you also build strength in yourself.

Evening Reflection: My Insights from Today

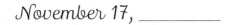

November 17, _____

Mental
Mindful attention to your sensations and breathing may help clarify
questions to ask that help you gain comfort and build self-confidence.

Spiritual
Claiming your inner power and trusting it is more essential
to your future than acting now.

Emotional
Although a strong action day, you may be emotionally vulnerable.
It is best to be cautious.

Physical
You are sensitive to others physically.
Take time to tune in to your body and know its limits.

Integration
Pressure you feel toward manifesting your intuitive understanding of things
and of people comes through your instinctive spiritual need to contribute
something of purpose and meaning to a larger whole. Use your own sense
of balance to monitor any emotional pulls you feel from others as you recognize how you feel internally vs. when with others who have emotions different from your own. You can set your own pattern of response and inner
response-ability when you recognize what feeds your creative awareness.

Evening Reflection: My Insights from Today

_____

_____

_____

_____

_____

_____

November 18, _____

Mental

Tap into your inner Self through meditation before speaking.
Remember that words carry messages from the subconscious as well as
from your personality. Be aware of how others may hear what you say.

Spiritual

Remembering past experiences help you clarify your perceptions.
When you replay old experiences, look for new awareness within them.

Emotional

You are open to others and highly sensitive to them.
Be sensitive and caring and include yourself in the equation.

Physical

Pay special attention to what your senses tell you.
They give you great information.

Integration

Cosmic laws of nature call forth your recollection of past experiences. These
experiences manifest in your current incarnation. When you tune in to your
deepest sense of Self, you feel gratification at the core of your being. Wait
patiently until you feel the stirrings within yourself of this deep sense of Self;
it comes through with a very gentle and soft voice that you hear whisper-
ing until it moves you without doubt or hesitation because you align to your
deepest Self. What you set in motion from this place of knowing can affirm
in mid-February for full manifestation. Trust yourself and avoid being pulled
by the emotions of others.

Evening Reflection: My Insights from Today

November 19, _____

Mental
Trying to explain what you feel may be difficult.
Mull things over for a few days until you feel clear.

Spiritual
Inner direction and power is essential to reaching your goals.
Wait until you have an inner vision of your direction.

Emotional
What you feel may reflect your inner process as much as that of others.

Physical
Let your body guide you instead of your mind.
Eat with discipline and exercise carefully so you avoid overindulgence.

Integration
While you may feel emotionally driven by the feelings and ideas of others, your own sense of certainty about your responses come into question. Stay alert for your own creative re-collections and higher Self to guide you. Trust that within a few days you will have a better perspective on yourself. Avoid any emotions that seem to be part of the external environment rather than ones that have deeper meaning. You are indeed empathic, picking up on what others feel even to the point that you may feel some physical discomforts like aches and pains that come and go. They are all part of the ebb and flow of the cosmic breath.

Evening Reflection: My Insights from Today

November 20, _____

Mental

Too much information may confuse you.
When you feel tension pay attention to the source of your tension.

Spiritual

Meditation with focus on your goals may relieve you of some tension.
Focus on the depth of your inner pool of awareness.

Emotional

Imagine you are unshakable in your trust of your instincts.
Perceive the world from this perspective.

Physical

You are highly sensitive to what is around you.
Breathe deeply and slowly to relax.

Integration

The sense of openness to others and to their feelings plays on you, shifting your feelings in accord with where you are and who you are with, despite your sense of wanting to feel anchored within. Avoid promises and commitments that may put pressure on you as such pressure is unhealthy just now. There is plenty of time for decisions and for patterns being established. Now is a time to consider options.

Evening Reflection: My Insights from Today

November 21, _____

Mental
It is a great day to spend time alone and to avoid the input of others.

Spiritual
Your internal world is key to your future. Listen to your inner voice that speaks in a whisper. It is a good day to hear what it says.

Emotional
The feelings of others may influence you in ways that you later regret.

Physical
When under stress you may push yourself to please other people.

Integration
Things may seem to be a good idea one minute and after a night's sleep you may wonder what you were thinking and why. Honor your confusion as part of a process of gaining clarity instead of allowing frustration to anchor within as part of your self-esteem. When feelings turn on and off within you, they express an inner process that activates your sensitivities toward acute alertness. Use such times for heightening your awareness. Make no long-term decisions.

Evening Reflection: My Insights from Today

November 22, _____

Mental
Energy follows thought.
Tap into your creative intelligence to make wise choices.

Spiritual
Take action based on what you know worked for you in the past.

Emotional
Consider the feelings of others, but honor your own feelings as well.

Physical
Emotional stress can result in physical depletion if you take on too much.

Integration
Tune in to your intuitive instincts despite any internal resistance you might feel in doing so. Pay special attention to how things smell to you. Record this information, at least internally. In addition, watch your responses to others very carefully. What you feel in the presence of others may tell you a great deal about how you are influenced by them. Store this information for later use, especially for when you are in social situations. Avoid too many commitments, despite any urges to do so.

Evening Reflection: My Insights from Today

November 23, _____

Mental
How well you align your thinking with the role you play
affects your self-esteem. Use your senses for information.

Spiritual
Stay in touch with animals and the way they communicate. Listen for "tells."

Emotional
Promising more than you can deliver puts you under stress, especially today.

Physical
Integrated physical activity is healthy as long as it balances you energetically.
Watch what you eat.

Integration
Action planned, or impulses felt are best envisioned and considered consciously before manifesting in reality (cf. Manifesting Generator Strategy). This process ensures outcomes most in line with what you wish. Since on a deep level of your being, you are open to others empathetically and emotionally, you may find that with self-reflective consideration what you would have done would have been uncomfortable for you while comfortable for others. Recognize your own Self while tuning in spiritually to a wider collective for action in the future. It is a time to assess relationships.

Evening Reflection: My Insights from Today

November 24, _____

Mental
You may feel confused by conflicting points of view
as you try to make sense of what is happening around you.

Spiritual
Stay compassionate and true to yourself despite the energy around you.

Emotional
Expressing emotions when reacting to circumstances may have consequences.
Be sensitive to building positive rather than negative energy.

Physical
Use your breathing to find equilibrium and operate from this balanced place.

Integration
Pay special attention to how those close to you motivate or de-motivate you.
Creative energy comes into play as you watch this process. Recognize how
others influence your motivation and instincts. What you learn about yourself today can help you navigate new patterns for yourself moving forward.
Avoid hasty actions. What do you know about your true Self now? And, when
living to your fullest, that's like what?

Evening Reflection: My Insights from Today

_____

_____

_____

_____

_____

_____

_____

_____

_____

November 25, _____

Mental
Your attention to details may make a difference
in how you interpret information.

Spiritual
Stay alert to nuances of behavior and of your deepest intentions.

Emotional
High sensitivity to the needs of others may move you
away from your own reactions. Pay attention.

Physical
Take yourself out of situations that put you under stress.
Your "nose knows."

Integration
Waiting for spiritual affirmation ideally continues before you take action
in your life, regardless of your impulse to take action. Waiting allows your
feelings to clarify and align with your wants, needs, and desires that have
basis in your life purpose rather than in the circumstances of your life at
the moment. Tune in to images of what can be accomplished through your
creative efforts, but pay attention to your thinking and to past experiences.

Evening Reflection: My Insights from Today

November 26, _____

Mental

Time is your friend in understanding your perceptions.
Wait for the inner stirrings of your mind to find confirmation in reality.

Spiritual

When you feel inner certainty resonating in your gut,
it most likely can be trusted.

Emotional

You are open to others now, so it is important that you wait for momentary
emotions to clear their influence from your perceptions.

Physical

Promises you make to others can put you under stress
mentally and physically.

Integration

You might feel pulled by groups of people as well as by individuals. When in
the presence of others, notice if you eat more than you would when alone.
Allow eating with others to be more of a ceremonial experience than just a
consumptive one. Remain open to your instinctive responses while you are
in social situations, and, at the same time, pay attention to your thoughts and
how they mirror the feelings of others as well as your own. Take inner action
instead of translating it to outward expression in action.

Evening Reflection: My Insights from Today

November 27, _____

Mental
Opinions are often best kept to yourself,
especially if they activate others in ways that may put you at risk.

Spiritual
Respect for yourself allows you to claim your full internal authority.
Align through meditation and focus.

Emotional
Those who value you fully, value your needs as much as their own.

Physical
Watch your digestion for signs of stress and use them to your benefit.

Integration
Outward actions are best considered when they align with what you know
about yourself and about what has worked well for you in the past. Taking
action when you are vulnerable to outside pressures can often cause you
stress later. Be mindful of your inner process, and use it as your authority while considering your creative options. When you care for yourself and
align to your highest desire, that's like what?

Evening Reflection: My Insights from Today

_____

_____

_____

_____

_____

_____

_____

_____

November 28, _____

Mental
Shifting energy creates mental stress that may cause you to second guess your understanding of things.

Spiritual
How you address challenges and stay balanced is key. Be patient, and continue to trust your process.

Emotional
Avoid input until you feel clarity yourself.

Physical
Get more rest than usual and avoid overexertion.

Integration
As you recognize patterns within your own being through your inner self-reflection, register your feelings and write them down if that helps you remember them. Note things in which you feel skilled. Consider enhancing those pursuits in the next three months. Stay with your spiritual process as well. If you have a focus for your spiritual endeavors, now is a good time to enhance those as well. Eat alone or with those who share a similar diet, if possible.

Evening Reflection: My Insights from Today

November 29, _____

Mental
Past actions based on your impulsive ideas,
if they are without strong foundations, may be risky today.

Spiritual
When what you know in your gut is familiar,
listen to it for its wisdom and use your creative intelligence wisely.

Emotional
You may have difficulty identifying your emotions, so take your time.

Physical
You are physically vulnerable to stress today. Be wary of overindulging.

Integration
The more aware you have been of influences others have on your emotional cycles, the more ability you have to secure your feelings in ways that enhance your spiritual experiences. It is all right to take charge of what you manifest, as long as this manifestation expresses your deep inner Self spiritually. It would be a misuse of your energy to spend it foolishly or in ways that dissipate it. Pay attention to those who enhance your life while moving back from those who deplete you.

Evening Reflection: My Insights from Today

November 30, _____

Mental

Details of your life circumstances may raise questions
about your self-direction and how you want to handle tasks-at-hand.

Spiritual

Call upon the depth of your intuition to align your life
with your greatest talents.

Emotional

When you feel at ease with others, you are likely to be at your best.

Physical

Take time to meditate and to focus on the still place within your depth. Breathe.

Integration

As you move through the day, notice differences in your energy level and be
mindful of what happened just before your energy shifted. Notice when you
are open to the physical feelings of others, and, at such times, how much
you are influenced by their moods. Watch how you operate. Take time for
self-reflection and meditate on what you want to have happen next in the
bigger picture of your life.

Evening Reflection: My Insights from Today

December 1, _____

Mental
Feeling passion for what you do allows you to complete
one cycle in your life before moving ahead.

Spiritual
When you master yourself and know your reality, you are likely to feel more at
ease in taking on a role you feel comfortable with in your life.

Emotional
Make sure to balance the *Axes of Awareness* (see resources on page 373),
or body/instinct/mind and feeling/instinct/mind, today.

Physical
Driving your body beyond its limits may be hard on your health.

Integration
The influence of people around you may impact you. Be mindful of what you
want to have happen before you take in the energy and input from others.
Use your inner resources to follow your intuitive voice. Pay attention to your
instincts and to smells you enjoy vs. the ones that repulse you. Keep your
sensitivity open so you perceive your own healthy direction.

Evening Reflection: My Insights from Today

_____

_____

_____

_____

_____

_____

_____

_____

_____

_____

December 2, _____

Mental
Stay on track with what you identified as your focus
and allow unexpected turns.

Spiritual
Use what you know about yourself and your process to guide you. Meditate.

Emotional
Be watchful for emotions triggered by circumstances.

Physical
Recognize your strengths and limitations physically,
and remember to watch your breath as a guide.

Integration
Questions about the meaning of your life and its purpose may surface today causing you to wonder what you are here for and whether any of the feelings you had in the past few weeks were real. Trust of yourself in each moment is crucial in progress for awareness. You flow in a natural way and right now your impulses may be pushing for expression based on responses to the circumstances around you and not necessarily to what is care-taking for your deepest Self as a unique entity. What do you want to have happen?

Evening Reflection: My Insights from Today

December 3, _____

Mental
Anchor ideas and possibilities of change through
mental recognition prior to action.

Spiritual
What you know about yourself and how you respond to things
is crucial in bringing change into your life.

Emotional
Past issues can be under the surface of awareness
and drive you toward missteps.

Physical
Take some time to take care of your body. Indulge your senses.

Integration
You may find yourself moving in directions of others while thinking you
are acting through your own clarity; you may, in actuality, be influenced by
the circumstances and feelings of others. It is still a time of openness on
the collective archetypal level of being, i.e., when we sleep we move into a
unity of consciousness. This openness creates vulnerability when it continues
throughout all layers of being. Make use of this sensitivity in yourself to think
about how you might best express your true spiritual Self. Avoid all impulsive
actions that originate in your emotions.

Evening Reflection: My Insights from Today

_____

_____

_____

_____

_____

_____

December 4, _____

Mental

Mental activity that stimulates you and other things you enjoy
can be highly rewarding today.

Spiritual

Stay quiet and meditate using your breathing
before taking action or making decisions.

Emotional

Use your mind to mediate feelings in order to avoid later problems.

Physical

Stay in environments that are comfortable for you today.

Integration

An important aspect of manifesting positively in your life resides in the
images you conceptualize and desire. What you think, you create. What you
desire, you charge emotionally with energy that then form images in your
mind. You have the capacity to transform your responses from the instinctive level of your being into higher cognitive concepts for manifestation. On
the empowered side this capacity produces great innovations in all fields of
human endeavor, while on the negative side it produces conflicts and disharmony. Recognize your own path spiritually and transform it through your
mental imagery.

Evening Reflection: My Insights from Today

December 5, _____

Mental
Balance how you spend your time to improve your sense of accomplishment.

Spiritual
You are open and empathic to others. Be sensitive to yourself also.

Emotional
It may be hard to tell what you want when others put pressure on you.

Physical
Make sure you get plenty of rest and alone time
in order to reduce stress today.

Integration
Pay attention to any situations in which you feel drained after the fact or in which you find that you are different when you are in the situation than when you're alone. This discernment tells you a great deal about the other person as well as about yourself. Use this information for your awareness and for building your strength within. Stay focused on your inner process and take extra time alone so you tune in to your inner voice clearly.

Evening Reflection: My Insights from Today

December 6, _____

Mental

Use this time to mull things over rather than to come to conclusions.

Spiritual

Stay focused on what is most important to you.
Keep your attention on your long-term goals.

Emotional

Stay attuned to the *Axes of Awareness* (see resources on page 373)
before reacting emotionally today.

Physical

Pay special attention to your breathing as a way to monitor stress.

Integration

Taking yourself out of situations that put you under pressure is essential in limiting your focus and bringing into perspective what is important to you. Ask yourself, "What do I want to have happen?" A clear inner vision is crucial to your future. Use your consciousness to build awareness within yourself. Time spent on this endeavor is time well spent.

Evening Reflection: My Insights from Today

December 7, _____

Mental
The viewpoint of other people may sway you in ways you will later regret.

Spiritual
Take extra meditation time to balance and find the still point within.
Doing this will help you stay balanced.

Emotional
Register what you feel without acting on it.

Physical
Eat with care and exercise with caution so you avoid depleting your energy.

Integration
Pressures of the day may trigger emotions. Be aware of your choices and of
what you actually want to have happen for yourself. It is always wise to pay
attention to your inner process and to under promise rather than over-promise
your time and energy. Take extra time to be alone and use past self-knowledge
to inform your current situations. Balance your body/instinct/mind and feel-
ing/instinct/mind, or *Axes of Awareness* (see resources on page 373).

Evening Reflection: My Insights from Today

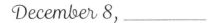

December 8, _____

Mental

Take time to reflect on all parts of your life today.
New awareness breakthroughs may surprise you.

Spiritual

Your inner voice is likely to be strong today.
Listen carefully to it and use it well.

Emotional

Before taking any action, breathe deeply and count to 10.

Physical

Make sure your commitments are ones you physically want to take on.

Integration

Expect some confusion between what you think and your instinctive responses. Confusion may be as simple as finding yourself eating something you know is less than ideal for you, or as complex as deciding how you might best care for someone else. The important point to remember is that you have many options; it takes time for you to truly know what you want for yourself. Although you may feel pulled to take action, wait for more auspicious action times. Take the time you need without rushing yourself. Pressure from others in your immediate environment create confusion between parts of yourself, especially if you give yourself reasons or come up with stories about what you should do and how you might best act.

Evening Reflection: My Insights from Today

December 9, _____

Mental
Take time to think about how you spend your resources
so you conserve them in all ways.

Spiritual
Caring for yourself takes that responsibility off others to do so.

Emotional
Balance your body/instinct/mind and feeling/instinct/mind
so you feel at ease.

Physical
Listen to your body carefully for what it tells you.
Considering its voice is important.

Integration
Many components turn on or off within you as the day sets up through the layers of your being. Such variance within the layers always tells a story of complex feelings both invigorating and exciting on one hand, and confusing or overwhelming on the other. The Manifesting Generating component of today requires visualizing careful plans prior to taking action. Any precipitous impulses or responses may lead in a direction that puts more pressure on you than you wish in the long run. Take your time. Clarify your direction as well as your experiences from the past as they feed into the present and set the course of manifestation for the future.

Evening Reflection: My Insights from Today

_____

_____

_____

_____

_____

_____

December 10, _____

Mental
Sudden insights about yourself may shift your thinking.

Spiritual
When you reframe your inner stories, you can make new choices.

Emotional
Watch inner responses when you are in emotional situations.
They give you information about yourself.

Physical
If you are vulnerable to emotional eating, today is a tricky day.

Integration
Call upon your intuition when considering your options and goals. Allow
yourself space to ask questions about what is important to you. When you
are empowered in yourself, that's like what? Take time to answer this question. Draw or make a note of your response. Then use some of the *Clean
Questions* (see resources on page 373) to deepen your understanding and
knowing. You will reap deep rewards and discover new inner resources.

Evening Reflection: My Insights from Today

December 11, _____

Mental
You may feel some new and challenging questions
for which you have no apparent answers.

Spiritual
Listening to your deepest Self is most crucial today,
despite feeling vulnerable to others.

Emotional
Be wary about doing things for other people's approval.

Physical
Pay special attention to your breathing today.

Integration
Although you are likely to feel a strong sense of inner knowing, take time to
connect with your deep instincts. Remember that you function in multiple
dimensions of time and space and are constantly in motion, just like the
cosmos. Take on only those tasks that you feel align with you and with your
goals. Err on the side of less is more so when you claim your power you do so
comfortably and confidently.

Evening Reflection: My Insights from Today

Mental

Conflicting thoughts and feelings may be confusing today.
Avoid confrontations.

Spiritual

Remain centered in the depth of your self-knowledge,
and remain in charge of your own destiny.

Emotional

Picking up on what others may feel can take you away from your own needs.
Use past experiences as a guide.

Physical

Strong body reactions alert you to what your physical reactions communicate.

Integration

Stay aware of pulls upon you from the collective that move you away from
your own recognition of Self because you feel empathy for others and for
their wellbeing. It is in your interest as well as in the interest of the wider
group to which you belong, i.e., humanity as a whole, that you pay attention
to the internal connection between your instinctive responses, your understanding, and your reasons for what you visualize and orchestrate. You are
the master of your destiny as well as that of the whole. Use your breath when
you meditate today; watch how it rules your capacity to move beyond your
mind and beyond words. Watch the breath as it gives you life. When you
speak, be aware of how the breath comes in to play.

Evening Reflection: My Insights from Today

December 13, _____

Mental
Body signals, properly interpreted, help guide you.

Spiritual
Stay attuned to all layers of your life
(Mental, Spiritual, Emotional, and Physical).
This sensitivity follows patterns you can recognize as healthy for you.

Emotional
Only express in action what you know has worked for you in the past.

Physical
Listen to your body and what it tells you.
Follow what you know is healthy for you.

Integration
Attending to your own feelings may allow you to avoid taking on more than you would wish in many spheres of your day-to-day world. Be with only those people with whom you truly feel comfortable and with whom you share experiences from the past. Such care may save you anxiety as well as stress. Social settings carry risks of pulling you in to things you may best avoid. Be mindfully alert.

Evening Reflection: My Insights from Today

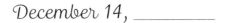

December 14, _____

Mental
Words carry energy that freeze feelings. Consider the consequences
and effects of your actions on yourself and others.

Spiritual
Internal changes manifest in actions over time.
Take time to meditate, and wait before you act.

Emotional
Emotional impulsiveness is a danger today.

Physical
Sensing what others feel may help you gauge the healthiest situations today. Eat
cautiously.

Integration
Pay attention to your body reactions until you find how you want to position yourself with respect to your life. Although the energy of the day may
push you toward action and you may indeed find action appropriate, you
will be well served to use past experiences to monitor your overt responses.
By monitoring emotions through awareness of body reactions, you may gain
perspective and find new ways that better balance you physically, resulting
in less body stress. Find the place inside you that remembers past body reactions in different situations. Apply these insights to your current life.

Evening Reflection: My Insights from Today

December 15, _____

Mental
Call upon past experiences before taking action today.

Spiritual
Inner awareness and meditation is essential to your balance.
Be gentle with yourself.

Emotional
Everyone may be under pressure today,
so be on alert for provoking emotions in others.

Physical
Pay attention to your eating today.
Remember to watch your breath as a way to monitor stress.

Integration
Pay special attention to the way you feel in terms of demands from others that end up making you feel depleted. When your inner voice whispers to you during your day, listen. Hear what your body tells you; if you feel stressed, pull back from the situation enough to gain perspective by recalling other times of similar stress. Is the stress coming from within you in terms of choices you made in the moment, or are they rooted in the demands others place upon you? Pressure to communicate with others in words carries risks today as well. Watch your communication with an eye to how others perceive what you say and turn it to meet their preconceived ideas. Be clear about your desires before you speak so you can clarify your wants, needs, and desires to others openly and honestly. Learn from past mistakes and move forward with optimism.

Evening Reflection: My Insights from Today

_____

_____

_____

_____

_____

_____

December 16, _____

Mental

Use past stories to identify what worked for you, and apply the knowledge now.

Spiritual

Build awareness of connections to others
without losing your perspective.

Emotional

Remember that when you feel valued and supported,
you feel positive self-worth.

Physical

Health is key to balance. Use your energy wisely today.

Integration

Allow your sense of what is correct to feed your instincts. Energy compatible with your understanding of things and about how you like to relate to others makes the difference in what works vs. what does not work for you as an individual. You are unique. Your needs are unique. Stay with your own healthy sense of Self as you tune in to your own connectivity to others. Recognize also that you pick up on the feelings of those around you and when you put yourself aside out of fear, or to please them, you do yourself a disservice. Stay true to your own inner sense of Self; your integrity of being requires this alignment within your being. Be wary of any promises you might make today. Stay open and flexible.

Evening Reflection: My Insights from Today

December 17, _____

Mental
Keep your goals in mind when you consider how to express yourself.

Spiritual
You are a multidimensional being who operates on many levels at once. Consider how to use your power for your highest purpose.

Emotional
When in doubt about things. Wait for clarity.

Physical
Body chemistry gives you subtle signals that help you adapt to your environment. Use all signals. Pay attention to your breathing.

Integration
Speak to those you care about regarding your feelings and how you might use your inner resources to best enhance your creative process. Feel your depth as well as the guiding principles in your life. What aspects of your health and/or wellbeing are enhanced by the way you live your life? What ways or patterns seem to diminish your sense of inner worth? What resources are augmented by your social context? Pay attention to all these issues today; you can use your past experiences to build for the future.

Evening Reflection: My Insights from Today

December 18, _____

Mental
How you interpret information impacts your worldview.
Consider how you can shift your perceptions to attain your goals.

Spiritual
You are the master of your mind.
Use dominion by attending to your inner Self.

Emotional
Saying "yes" when you want to say "no" undermines your self-esteem.

Physical
Balancing the *Axes of Awareness* (see resources on page 373) is crucial to health.

Integration
While you move through your day, pay attention to how others challenge your perceptions. At the same time, stay tuned in to your own intuitive depth of being so you recognize your aligned energy and how you feel when you pick up on the feelings or health of others. Social pulls can move you away from your own process. Guard against taking on things; you have the capacity to take things on, but make sure they reflect your feelings. Words have power. Use them carefully to express the truth you find within as it rings true in your deep Self.

Evening Reflection: My Insights from Today

December 19, _____

Mental

Review stories you tell about your life to others.
They reveal much about your self-perceptions.

Spiritual

Meditate. Focus on how you have progressed in self-awareness this year.

Emotional

Be very watchful about extending yourself too much.

Physical

Rest, despite pressure on you to do more.

Integration

The ebb and flow of the cosmic energy pattern gives us the potential to trust our inner rhythm as a guide in leading us toward self-realization and self-recognition. Precipitous action often takes us in directions that need adjustment later. However, when we second-guess ourselves, day-to-day doubt and fear replace confidence in explorations. Talk about your feelings with others to help sort through your inner feelings. Nevertheless, be wary of letting others influence you with their own needs, wants, and desires. Use your breathing as a guide to how well you tune in to your spiritual alignment with your current instinctive sense of what is correct for you in your current circumstances. Avoid decisions for the next week while things settle within and give you confirmation of your ideal path.

Evening Reflection: My Insights from Today

Mental

Remain alert to opportunities that integrate and align your long-term goals.

Spiritual

Letting go of all the "noise" distracting you from inner clarity is essential.

Emotional

Avoid emotional situations that seem to undervalue you.

Physical

Your stamina and physical energy throughout the day reflects your health.

Integration

Think about how you can imagine re-crafting your past into an idyllic picture. Create it. Now think of it with the individuals involved in the setting harmoniously enjoying social interaction; then imagine the smells in the air and the harmony in your body; next hear the voices in your head as you imagine the conversations or the music of the tones of the voices around you. Put these positive images in your mind and return to them, at least for the next week, daily. As you align the images over the next week into a positive picture, the planetary influences in your body will anchor them into place and begin creating a new reality in form. Allow the universe to care for you now. Relax and breathe with it.

Evening Reflection: My Insights from Today

December 21, _____

Mental
Take information in as data. Build hypotheses rather than conclusions.

Spiritual
Balance in all areas of life aligns you to your inner core.
Be alert to your inner needs.

Emotional
Moods often transparently reflect levels of integrated balance.
Use the clues.

Physical
Your body tells you if you are in or out of balance
in subtle and in obvious ways.

Integration
Self-awareness about how you balance the Four Worlds, Mental, Spiritual, Emotional, and Physical, in your life determines the way you manifest yourself in the world at any moment in time. Orient yourself toward expression of your highest Self in the world. Rise to the part you play. Dress in character. Move in character. Create your Self-expression in a way that meets your true nature and values. Today builds your depth of purpose. Set it up so 20 years from now you will look back and be glad you made the choices you are making now. Enjoy yourself. Experience its Power.

Evening Reflection: My Insights from Today

_____

_____

_____

_____

_____

_____

_____

December 22, _____

Mental
How you think reflects your inner balance. Be mindful and thoughtful.

Spiritual
Deep inner knowing that moves you to action may be all right.

Emotional
Recognize your intuitive instincts, and use them with intelligence.

Physical
Emotions run high for everyone today and can put you under physical stress.

Integration
Your expression of Self in the world is influenced by the way you perceive the union of body/mind/instinct and feeling/mind/instinct. Take a mental photo of yourself and recognize yourself from the other person's perspective. Allow your nature to shine so it shares the basic value of human survival. Look forward as well as backward in order to appreciate the development of your life along its path, and recognize that the alignment you have sought in all dimensions of your being have brought you to your current moment, perfect in itself. If you are breathing and reading you have the capacity to use your mind to enjoy your full Self. Be with your potential now.

Evening Reflection: My Insights from Today

December 23, _____

Mental
Your behavior affects how you are perceived.
Be mindful what you do and how you think.

Spiritual
You are highly sensitive to others
and may feel more vulnerable today than usual.

Emotional
Consider the way things will play out over the next several days,
prior to taking action.

Physical
Exercise with care, and remember to eat and drink properly for your body.

Integration
Once you recognize the difference within your own consciousness between perceptual reality and the truth of the multidimensional layers on which you function, you gain a great sense of relationship coming from within. Several components of the multidimensional charts show the possibility right now to recognize this unifying thread holding all our layers together as connected, yet individual, beings. Step outside the usual boundaries of awareness with understanding and caring, and step into your true Self.

Evening Reflection: My Insights from Today

December 24, _____

Mental

If you have been considering something for a while,
you might want to consider taking action.

Spiritual

It is a good day to feel your strength
and congratulate yourself on your growth.

Emotional

Express your deepest feelings to those you love.

Physical

Enjoy your physical health, and treat it with mindful indulgence.

Integration

Love yourself as much as you love anyone else. Move yourself inward toward
spiritual harmony with your inner process. Align with your life manifestation
by orienting your emotions in transformational ways. Be your best Self. Allow
the cosmic dance in which you move to gracefully guide your future. Breathe
the air with gratitude for its abundance as you nurture those who nurture
you, including the Earth. Recognize today, your unity with others and how
deeply connected you are to them. You are vulnerable and emotionally sensitive so be cognizant of who and what affects you. Utilize your resources to
their fullest to manifest the grace and power.

Evening Reflection: My Insights from Today

December 25, _____

Mental
Inner self-talk helps you balance all parts of yourself.
Use words with consciousness.

Spiritual
Call upon past stories that you learned from
to enhance your positive self-regard.

Emotional
Find a place of emotional balance within,
and anchor yourself there when with others.

Physical
Take time to be alone to rejuvenate and recharge your energy.

Integration
Your desires, based on your reflection of past experiences, give you some sense of authority to speak from within. Feel secure when you know deeply and from yourself; remain seeking answers when you know deeply that you do not know from the Self. Journey forward to find full clarity. It is always available with a bit of focus and inner stillness.

Evening Reflection: My Insights from Today

December 26, _____

Mental
Consider all parts of yourself before you take action.

Spiritual
Give permission to yourself to align with your highest aspirations and values.

Emotional
Emotional stress amplifies itself to gain attention.

Physical
Exercise and eat with great discipline. Avoid social eating.

Integration
Those people with whom you feel relaxed and stress free are those with whom you can best communicate. If you feel any doubts within your gut, wait. You are always able to be of most service when you come from an internal place of clarity and inner aligned balance. By checking facts and making sure that you have inner clarity and balance, you are able to set an intention free of assumptions and predisposing biases. Use Clean Language questions to go deep, and clear any metaphoric patterns that slant your perspective.

Evening Reflection: My Insights from Today

December 27, _____

Mental
Your mind and viewpoint significantly affect your sense of balance and joy. Let your mind serve you.

Spiritual
Meditation is essential to gain perspective of your part in a greater whole.

Emotional
A single standard for yourself and others reflects inner congruence.

Physical
Use subtle signals from your body to indicate where and how you are vulnerable.

Integration
Stay tuned in to your known parameters of comfort: eat your ideal diet, meditate, breathe through the stress of others, exercise carefully so you do not hurt yourself or your muscles, show compassion and openness to others without sacrificing your own Self. The more you pay attention to the running commentary in your mind, monitoring it and censoring it towards positive expression within the boundaries of reality, the better balanced you will be. Premature action is never worth the risk of its consequences. Take your time. If you feel at all uncertain about anything today, take time to sleep on it. Patience pays dividends.

Evening Reflection: My Insights from Today

December 28, _____

Mental
How you use your mind makes a difference in how you feel. Pay attention.

Spiritual
Although you have penetrating awareness and strong intuition today,
you may also feel some self-doubt.

Emotional
The feelings of others may put pressure on you to act impulsively.
Be cautious.

Physical
Take time to register your body sensations before you make any decisions.

Integration
Inner balance and alignment are key to manifesting what you want to have
happen in the future. You co-create your future with your inner story, so the
clearer you are, the more congruently what you want to create manifests.
Everyone ultimately is here to manifest their highest Self in the world. You
are unique and divine. Stay in touch with your highest Self and use your
awareness and sensitivity to manifest your true Self.

Evening Reflection: My Insights from Today

December 29, _____

Mental
Take time to rest by becoming involved in things that align deeply with you.

Spiritual
You are intuitively sensitive to what serves your higher Self. Honor it.

Emotional
Know that there are times when you are best served
by pulling your energy within.

Physical
Respect your physical boundaries and limitations with discipline and thanks.

Integration
Continue meditating, and now add in to the mix of your meditation consideration of those things in your life that allow you to feel a sense of connection to what seems most deeply connected to you. Finding a sense of balance within oneself for inner relatedness to the wellbeing of Self and others allows one to feel a sense of inner dominion. As you continue your process of clarifying your inner instinct as it relates to a wider sense of purpose for you, also feel how in tune you feel with a stronger sense of confidence in what you can achieve. Remember always that you have your own purpose in this life. No one else carries the same path. Avoid too many social commitments; they may pull you away from your own feelings and desires.

Evening Reflection: My Insights from Today

December 30, _____

Mental
Bringing into action what you have been thinking about for a while may be important to you today.

Spiritual
Make sure that any action you take honors your deepest values.

Emotional
Be firm in your actions but cautious and gentle in your attitude.

Physical
Look for physical "tells" that may reveal what you really feel and value.

Integration
Imagine balance you believe to be ideal for you. Within a couple of days you should feel intuitive confirmation of your direction with a deep sense of affirmation in your gut. Make an effort to think outside your usual way of thinking. Feel the strength of others pulling you in their directions, and yet, feel the strength of your inner resolve to balance your needs, wants, and desires in healthy ways.

Evening Reflection: My Insights from Today

December 31, _____

Mental
Use this last day of the year to reflect on your progress
and to congratulate yourself on challenges you have overcome.

Spiritual
Reflect on the direction you are taking, and meditate on it to gain clarity.

Emotional
Envision possibilities and how they might come to fruition.

Physical
Take time to rest and regroup physically.

Integration
Take the day for inner evaluation of where you are in your life. Consider
the way you express your role in the world. Are the perceptions of others
congruent with your perception of Self? Are there ways you consistently feel
misperceived? Review the stories of your life. When you meet someone for
the first time, what do you describe about yourself? How do you present
yourself? What picture do you paint for them to look at regarding you and
your life? Stories told reflect deeply on the view you have, since your mind
tells about and repeats patterns that manifest in your life.

Evening Reflection: My Insights from Today

Acknowledgments

$\mathcal{I}$n 1999, Ra Uru Hu asked me to scientifically validate the Human Design System. My statistical research on 30,000 cases confirmed that the Body Map was valid in showing Five Different Ways of Being, or Types. These Five Types show how cosmic energy impacts you and moves you toward manifesting in the Mental World. However, I also determined that the Human Design System did not hold up scientifically and disseminated misinformation.

As a social science researcher, I continued my statistical research by expanding calculations to include critical times in Human Development during the first three months of life. My expanded work includes how you function in all Four Worlds, the Mental, Emotional, Spiritual, and Physical Worlds, over six months when your development is crucial to interacting, perceiving, and relating to the world around you.

Over more than 20 years, my work expanded as I validated my research clinically on 15,000 cases. This work has been intense and eye-opening. I discovered that working with the Four Worlds and how those worlds integrate with consciousness dramatically changes what the Energy Maps show. They show that manifesting your highest potential by combining the Four Worlds is your birthright. They also show your strengths and vulnerabilities, your life purpose, how you make decisions and many other things.

Over the years, I often felt overwhelmed by the breadth of this work and have been blessed to have the help of an extraordinary team working tirelessly with me. Marvin Portner, my dear husband, soul mate, and fellow traveler, is always by my side, encouraging me in my work and buoying me up when I feel discouraged.

Cindy O'Connor Smith recognized the value of my work in 2007 and has been a supporter and co-creator with me since then. Cindy has helped create many of the materials I imagined. She is a dear, faithful friend, fellow traveler, and inspiration to me. I know she and I have a God-given mission to bring truth and awareness to our audience while honoring the integrity of Noble Energy knowledge.

Charles E. Haspel coded the statistical research on the Human Design System and has been a constant support and computer consultant. We owe an outstanding debt of gratitude to Charles for designing a database for me to use when writing the Cosmic Guidance statements in each world. Without Charles' technical skills, much of my work would not have come to fruition.

Michelle M. White implemented the design of my books, *Astrology Essentials, Cosmic Secrets, First-Degree Reiki Manual, Second-Degree Reiki Manual and Workbook,* and this book, *Cosmic Guidance for Mastering Your Life.* Michelle is a pleasure to work with and always brings a sharp eye and design skills that make my writing better than it would be without her help. I am very grateful that she is on my team.

Melanie Herschorn guided my thinking and way of presenting material. She encourages me when I need encouragement and helps me verbalize complex concepts in understandable ways. Melanie is a true blessing.

Erin Keller posts on social media and creates beautiful posts from my materials and writings. Her ability to capture the essence of my work is brilliant, and her help allows me to expand my reach beyond what I could do alone. Erin is a pleasure to work with and also a true blessing.

Nick Lush works with me on coding and editing the plethora of my writing. His attention to nuance and detail is admirable. Nick has been a supportive friend and loyal employee for many years. He is an invaluable member of our team.

To all my clients and webinar participants, I am deeply honored and grateful to have your trust. *Cosmic Guidance for Mastering Your Life* can change your life for the better. I sincerely hope that you work with the Four Worlds, and recognize that you are a multidimensional being of light here to manifest your highest potential. Do your inner work and be who you are here to be.

In Loving Light,
Dr. Eleanor
Mount Pleasant, South Carolina
November 2023

Tools and Resources
for Mastering Your Life

Throughout *Cosmic Guidance for Mastering Your Life* there are references to resources and tools that enhance growth in consciousness and help you understand and work with the Four Worlds.

Go to https://www.nobleenergywellness.com/cosmic-guidance/ for the following helpful resources:

- Assessing Your Core Values
- Build a Strong Sense of Self
- Clean Questions
- Empowered Self-talk
- Glossary
- Gratitude in the Four Worlds
- SMART Goals
- The Axes of Awareness
- Transformational Synthesis

About the Author

$\mathcal{I}$t is my great honor and privilege to share my knowledge with you and to use it to help you live a life of fulfillment and recognition of your divinity.

My interest in astrology began in 1971 when I was told that astrology is the most scientific of the esoteric disciplines. At the time, I had just completed my doctorate at the University of Chicago, was well versed in psychology, sociology, anthropology, and biology, and had done extensive research on world religions; however, hearing that astrology was scientific intrigued me.

I found an astrology bookstore near my home and proceeded to learn how to calculate an astrology chart. It proved to be the hardest thing I had ever attempted to learn. The language was symbolic and the mathematical calculations complex. But I persisted and began to understand basic astrological work.

Two years later, I was deeply honored and blessed to book an astrological reading with Katherine de Jersey. The reading with her showed me the power and depth of astrology in the hands of a Master. I studied astrology privately with several astrologers and was also in training as a Jungian

Analyst. I also focused on Kundalini energy and meditation because I was having Kundalini energy experiences, and I wanted to understand them and my psychic abilities.

In 1996, I encountered the Human Design Mandala, a complex, yet intriguing system that intertwines psychology, astrology, and developmental science. My fascination with the Human Design System deepened with each passing year.

Through my research, I had a staggering revelation: 99% of humanity possesses the inherent potential to manifest their true selves. Tragically, the majority of people remain oblivious to the existence of the Four Worlds — the Mental, Spiritual, Emotional, and Physical dimensions that govern our daily reality.

While their lack of awareness is not inherently "bad," it is a missed opportunity for growth and fulfillment. When individuals are unaware of the Four Worlds, they navigate life without understanding the diverse dimensions of their consciousness. They may feel disconnected, struggling to align actions with their true selves, and miss out on the profound impact that recognizing and harmonizing with these dimensions can have on their overall wellbeing.

It was then that my mission crystallized in my mind: to illuminate these dimensions, to guide individuals towards a conscious existence that embraces the essence of their soul.

Noble Energy Wellness™

Noble Energy Wellness focuses on Energy Medicine and Holistic options for healing and health. Dr. Marvin and Dr. Eleanor teach energy wellness in their weekly Manifest Your Dreams Webinar. Through the webinar, you can learn how to live authentically while manifesting your actual potential by understanding and integrating the Four Worlds into your daily life. Register to learn how you can manifest your dreams by attending these weekly webinars.
https://www.nobleenergywellness.com

Noble Energy Maps™

Noble Energy Maps focus on Dr. Eleanor's proprietary and innovative system for mapping how cosmic energy impacted you during your childhood development and how you can use this knowledge to optimally time your decisions, identify your life purpose, and live a self-realized life. Dr. Eleanor statistically validated her system through over 45,000 cases and uses Noble Energy Maps to guide clients toward wholeness and empowerment.
https://www.nobleenergywellness.com/energy-map/

The Noble Logo has a special place in Dr. Eleanor's heart. Her first cat, Noble, lived to age 22 and was an inspiration and guide during important times in Dr. Eleanor's growth and studies. He worked with her and Dr. Marvin when they hosted weekend groups for over ten years. Noble always helped guide them toward whom to work with next, as well as to the area that clients needed to work on. Dr. Eleanor uses calculations based on research done on her two homegrown twin kittens.

The critical human developmental times used in Dr. Eleanor's proprietary maps, have proven accurate clinically and statistically, which map the Four Worlds in your energy field and how you can best function.

The Mandala of Synthesis describes the elements coded into Dr. Eleanor's proprietary Noble Energy Maps. The Mandala of Synthesis includes the Kabalistic Tree of Life, Chakras, Astrology, the Hexagrams of the I-Ching, and critical times in early Human Development. Dr. Eleanor calculates her maps and integrates the information coded into a graphic illustrating the way you use your energy, where the flow of energy becomes clear. Dr. Eleanor's extensive education as a social scientist, researcher, and clinician has empowered her to formulate a complete system that recognizes the complexity of your consciousness and shows how you can best use it for growth and expansion of consciousness.

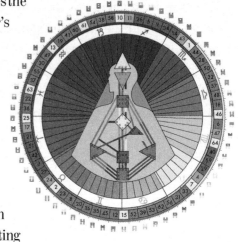

https://www.nobleenergywellness.com/mandala-of-synthesis

Printed in Great Britain
by Amazon

41775486R00218